DAFFY DICTIONARY

FUNABRIDGED DEFINITIONS
from
AARDVARK
to
ZUIDER ZEE

by Joseph Rosenbloom
illustrations by Joyce Behr

 STERLING PUBLISHING CO., INC. NEW YORK

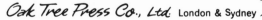
Oak Tree Press Co., Ltd. London & Sydney

BY THE SAME AUTHOR

Biggest Riddle Book in the World
Doctor Knock-Knock's Official Knock-Knock Dictionary

OTHER BOOKS OF INTEREST

Calculator Puzzles, Tricks and Games   Eye Teasers
Code Games   Would You Believe . . . ?
The Curious Book   Would You Believe This, Too?

To Lisa Schechtman

Copyright © 1977 by Joseph ROSENBLOOM

Published 1977 by Sterling Publishing Co., Inc.
419 Park Avenue South, New York, N.Y. 10016
Distributed in Australia and New Zealand by Oak Tree Press Co., Ltd.,
P.O. Box J34, Brickfield Hill, Sydney 2000, N.S.W.
Distributed in the United Kingdom and elsewhere in the British Commonwealth
by Ward Lock Ltd., 116 Baker Street, London W 1
Manufactured in the United States of America
All rights reserved
Library of Congress Catalog Card No.: 76-51173
Sterling ISBN 0-8069- 4542-7 Trade   Oak Tree 7061-2544-4
4543-5 Library

Introduction

Parents and teachers have for generations sought ways of training the child to make better use of the dictionary. The present book takes a fresh look at the problem. In my view, much of what the child learns is gained in the course of play activities. Motor skills, to use an obvious example, are developed in the course of physical play. In much the same way, language skills are acquired during wordplay.

If one looks closely at the different kinds of jokes children tell each other, much of the humor is seen to be based on wordplay. The humor turns on the fact that words have multiple meanings, that sound and spelling are not necessarily linked, or that language is riddled with semantic traps into which the unwary can easily be led. Young people get a great kick out of discovering and experimenting with just such vagaries of language. They may not be aware of it, but while they are laughing they are learning much about the properties of language and meaning. Truly serious learning is going on underneath the chuckles.

A child with some experience in wordplay activities is already initiated into some of the intricacies of language. When he goes to a regular dictionary for information, he is not intimidated by the problems he is apt to encounter. This Daffy Dictionary may therefore serve as an introduction to a serious dictionary.

Many different kinds of wordplay are incorporated in this book. One type involves taking the word apart:

Amidst
A thick fog.

Another kind depends on the fact that a single word may have more than one meaning:

Band-aid
A fund for needy musicians.

Or the joke may be based on homonyms:

Conceit
A case of *I* (eye) strain.

Still another type uses words that sound almost alike, but not quite. This is made easier when the definition is embodied in a proverb or common expression:

Diet
A case of mind over platter.

Finally, epigrams or witty sayings are included because they express perceptive ideas in a neat, amusing way:

Gossip
A person who will never tell a lie—if the truth will do more damage.

To help the young reader "get" the joke, the key word to each pun is given in parenthesis. A pronunciation guide is used where needed. The pronunciation guide uses ordinary letters in place of special diacritical marks.

In addition to the types of wordplay previously mentioned, the present book uses any short humor form that can be cast as a definition. There are puns, proverbs, gags, riddles, aphorisms, quips, etc. I hope that the sheer variety will make the book more enjoyable as well as a more useful educational tool.

JOSEPH ROSENBLOOM

To the Reader

To use most dictionaries, you have to know how to spell the word first in order to find what you are looking for. In this dictionary, what helps is to know what the word really means. If you don't get the joke, look up the word in a regular dictionary. Remember, there are all kinds of jokes in this book. Once you know the real meaning of the word, you will understand the joke better. Of course, if you still don't get it, maybe it's just a bad joke.

If you want to find all the jokes on one subject —monsters, for instance—look it up in the index. The index puts all the same subjects together into categories so you can find them quicker and more easily.

aardvark
(ARD-vark) Aan aanimal thaat resembles the aanteater.

abalone
(ab-e-LOW-nee) An expression of disbelief. (*agh, baloney!*)

abash
(uh-BASH) A big party.

abdomen
(AB-doh-men) Men from the invisible planet Abdo.

abominable snowman
A pesty Eskimo.

absurdity
(ab-SUR-di-tee) Any opinion that differs from your own.

abundance
(a-BUN-duns) A social event in the bakery.

Abu-Ac

abut
(a-BUT) The unsmoked end of a cigar or cigarette.

acacia
(a-KAY-sha) In the event that. Ex: Acacia *(in case you)* don't know, you're stepping on my foot.

accomplish
(uh-KOM-plish) A partner in crime. *(accomplice)*

accord
(a-KORD) A thick piece of string.

accordance
(a-KOR-duns) A piece of string doing the twist.

account
The husband of a countess.

accountants
(a-KOWNT-ants) Old accountants never die, they just lose their balance.

accrue
(a-KROO) The people who run a ship.

acorn
Something caused by a tight shoe.

acoustic
(a-KOO-stik) A stick used to play billiards. *(a cue stick)*

acquaint
(a-KWAYNT) Something old fashioned. Ex: She is acquaint *(a quaint)* old lady.

acquaintance
(a-KWAYNT-uns) Someone you know well enough to borrow from, but not well enough to lend to.

acquire
(a-KWYRE) A group of people who sing together. *(a choir)*

actor
Someone who would rather have a small role than a long loaf.

Acu-Ad

acute pain
A pretty window.

Adam
The one person in the world who could not truthfully say, "Pardon me, haven't I met you before?"

addition
What a dining table has. *(a dish on)*

address
Something worn by girls and women.

adhesive tape
A sticky cassette.

ad-lib
A liberation movement for television commercials.

administer
(ad-MIN-i-ster) A high government official in charge of advertising.

ado
(a-DOO) What the bride and groom say to the minister.

adobe
(a-DOH-bee) A stinging insect made out of flour and water. *(a dough bee)*

adolescence
(ad-ah-LESS-ens) The time when a girl begins to powder and a boy begins to puff.

adore
Entrance to a house.

adult
A person who has stopped growing at both ends and now is growing in the middle.

advertising
The art of making you believe you've longed all your life for something you never heard of before.

affix
(a-FIKS) Big, big trouble.

afford
A well-known car.

after-dinner mint
What you need in an expensive restaurant when the waiter hands you the check.

aftermath
The period following algebra.

Ah-Al

ahem
The edge around a skirt or dress.

Alabama elephants
Elephants whose Tuscaloosa. *(tusks are looser)*

alarm clock
(1) A device to scare the living daylights into you.
(2) A convenient invention if you like that sort of ting. (3) Eye opener.

align
(a-LYNE) A straight geometric figure.

alimony
(AL-e-moh-nee) The high cost of leaving.

allegro
(a-LEG-roh) A chorus line. *(a leg row)*

alligator pear
A crocodile couple. *(alligator pair)*

all-star show
A performance one can see in a planetarium.

allure
(a-LYOORE) A device used in catching fish.

ally
(a-LYE) An untruth.

aloha
(a-LOH-a) Reduced in sound. Ex: Please speak in aloha *(a lower)* voice, or you'll wake the baby.

alphabet soup
Eating your own words.

already
Completely crimson in color. *(all red)*

alternation
(AWL-ter-nay-shun) A country that prays in church a good deal of the time. *(altar nation)*

amateur
(am-e-TOOR) To be available. Ex: Amateur *(I'm at your)* service, madam.

amateur show
"Maim That Tune."

Amazon
(AM-a-zon) Claiming to be a child of. Ex: Amazon *(I'm a son)* of a gun!

ambition
(am-BISH-un) A get ahead-ache.

Amb-An

ambulance
A crash and carry motor vehicle.

ambushed
(AM-busht) To be totally exhausted. Ex: I really ambushed *(am bushed)* after a day at school.

amenable
(a-MEE-ne-bl) A steer with a nastier disposition. *(a meaner bull)*

amidst
A thick fog.

amount
A horse for riding.

amphibians
(am-FIB-ee-enz) Animals that tell lies.

angel
A heavenly creature that is always harping on something or other.

animal cracker
(AN-uh-mal KRAK-er) A lion tamer's whip.

annex
(a-NEKS) A former girl or boyfriend. *(an ex)*

announce
Exactly one-sixteenth of a pound.

annual
(AN-yoo-ul) A command issued in a stern voice. Ex: Annual *(And you will)* do as I say, or else!

ant
An insect that works hard but still finds time to go to all the picnics.

anteater
A cannibal. *(aunt eater)*

anthem
Rather goodlooking. Ex: Tall, dark and anthem *(handsome)*.

antidotes
(AN-tee-dotes) A female relative showing love for her niece or nephew. Ex: My uncle likes me very much, but my antidotes on me.

antifreeze
(an-tee-FREEZ) What happens to your aunt when you steal her blanket.

Antiq-Ap

antiquate
Aunt Katherine. *(auntie Kate)*

antique
(an-TEEK) Something one generation buys, the next generation gets rid of, and the following generation buys again.

antlers
Deer don't have uncles, just antlers.

apiary
(AY-pee-er-ee) The monkey house in the zoo.

aplomb
(a-PLOM) A small, sweet fruit. *(a plum)*

apostle
A package from home. *(a parcel)*

apparent
A mother or a father.

appeal
The outer covering of a fruit.

appear
A long dock for boats. *(a pier)*

apricot
Where an ape sleeps. *(ape cot)*

April showers
Important events in American history—they brought the Mayflowers.

arcade
The drink served on Noah's boat.

archaic
(ar-KAY-ik) Dessert made of flour, sugar and eggs. Ex: We can't have archaic *(our cake)* and eat it too.

arch criminal
Someone who robs shoe stores.

archeologist
(ar-kee-AHL-e-jist) A man whose career lies in ruins.

architect
Noah's profession.

Arctic explorer
Someone who believes the snow is whiter on the other side.

Arg-Arr

argument
A discussion in which two people try to get the last word in first.

arithmetic
A subject that is hard work because of all the numerals you have to carry.

armor plate
Dishes that knights ate from.

aroma
On to the capital of Italy!

arrears
(a-REERS) What we listen with. Ex: Friends, Romans, countrymen, lend me arrears *(your ears)*.

arrest
The time you take off for relaxation.

arrival
(uh-RYE-vuhl) A competitor. *(a rival)*

arrowhead
A real sharp guy.

arson
What parents call their male offspring. *(our son)*

art gallery
Hall of frame.

arthritis
Twinges in the hinges.

artificial
The judge at an art show. *(art official)*

artificial respiration
Most people who have tried artificial respiration prefer the real thing.

artists
People who can draw more than their breath.

ascent
(a-SENT) A copper coin worth one-hundredth part of a dollar.

Asia Minor
An oriental youth.

Asian flu
Part of a Chinese chimney.

aspire
The tall, pointed top of a church.

Asp-At

aspirin
A drug on the market.

assail
An opportunity to buy bargains.

asset
(ASS-et) A little donkey.

astronaut
(AS-truh-nawt) A person who has to be fired before he can work.

astronomer
A night watchman with a college degree.

athlete's tongue
A condition caused by putting your foot in your mouth once too often.

Atlas
Probably the greatest thief in history. He held up the whole world.

atom
The man who went around with Eve. *(Adam)*

atomic ache
What you get if you swallow too much uranium.

atomic bomb
What makes molehills out of mountains.

atomic war
A time when all men are cremated equal.

attire
(a-TIRE) Something round, rubbery and filled with air. *(a tire)*

attraction
What one magnet feels for another.

auction
(AWK-shun) A place where you get something for nodding.

auctioneer
Someone who looks forbidding.

austere
(aw-STEER) Guide the course of. Ex: You can either sink austere *(or steer)* the boat.

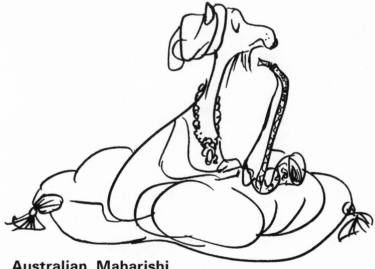

Australian Maharishi
A kanguru.

Aut-Ax

autobiography
  The life story of a car.

autumn
  The season when it is easiest to read books because then nature turns the leaves.

avail
  What a bride wears on her head. *(a veil)*

avenue
  To possess something you never had before. Ex: We avenue *(have a new)* baby at home.

average person
  A minority group. Few people admit they are average.

aviary
  (AY-vee-er-ee) In a high degree. Ex: Having aviary *(a very)* good time, wish you were here.

avoidable
  (a-VOYD-a-bl) What a matador tries to do. *(avoid a bull)*

avowal
  (a-VOW-ul) a, e, i, o, u and sometimes y.

awry
  (a-RYE) A kind of bread. *(a rye)*

axe
  A chopstick.

B-B gun
A very small or young rifle. *(baby gun)*

baa-baa
The man who gives sheep their haircuts. *(barber)*

baby
Mother's little yelper.

babysitter
Someone who is paid to sit on babies.

bachelor
A man who never Mrs. anyone.

bacilli
(ba-SIL-ee) Foolish or stupid: Ex: "Don't bacilli *(be silly),*" said one germ to the other.

back down
The tail feathers of a duck.

bacteria
(bak-TEER-ee-a) The rear entrance to a cafeteria.

bad comedian
A person who can't even entertain a thought.

Bad-Ban

bad guy
Someone who, on the sands of time, leaves only heel marks.

baker
A person who kneads the dough.

bakery customer
Someone who takes the cake.

balderdash
(BAWL-der-dash) A short line with less hair.

baldness
The perfect cure for dandruff.

ball game
A contest to see who can cry the loudest. *(bawl game)*

banana
A fruit with a split personality.

banana peel
A golden slipper.

band-aid
A fund for needy musicians.

bandit
An outlaw strong enough to hold up stagecoaches.

bandleader
Someone who has to face the music.

banker
Someone who is unhappy if he loses interest.

bankruptcy
(BANK-rupt-see) A fate worse than debt. *(death)*

banks
Where rivers keep their money.

barbarism
(BAH-bah-riz-em) Strong beliefs held by elephants. *(Babar-ism)*

Barbary pirate
Someone who cuts people's hair and then charges them too much.

barber
(1) Someone who goes through life getting in other people's hair. (2) The one person to whom everyone takes off his hat.

barber shop
A clip joint.

Bare-Bas

barefooted criminal
  A heel without a sole *(soul)*.

barium
  (BAR-ee-um) What is done to the dead. *(bury 'um)*

baroque
  (ba-ROHK) To be without a cent. Ex: I'd lend you some money, but I'm baroque *(broke)* myself.

baseball bat
  A fly swatter.

baseball diamond
  The biggest jewel in the world.

baseball stadium
  A cool place because of all the fans.

bashful
Describing a banged-up car.

basketball player
Someone who can dribble all the time and still be neat.

bass
A fish with a deep voice.

bath
The surest way to get into hot water.

bathing beauty
A girl worth wading for.

bathtub
A noisy place because of all the rings.

beach
A place where people slap you on the back and ask how you are peeling.

bear
If you must hunt bear *(bare)*, it would be wise to avoid drafts.

beatnik
Santa Claus the day after Christmas.

beauty contest
A lass *(last)* roundup.

beauty mark
An "A" in math.

beauty parlor
A place where women curl up and dye.

Bed-Bet

bed
A piece of furniture which gets larger at night when two feet are added to it.

bedbug
An undercover agent.

bee
An insect that knows how to make a point.

bees
The cause of hives.

befoul
To be a chicken, turkey, goose, duck, etc.

begat
(bee-GAT) A large head covering. *(big hat)*

beginning
The inning that decides the ballgame.

behavior
To weigh more than something else. *(be heavier)*

belt
It is better to tighten it than to lose your pants.

Bermuda shorts
Pygmies who live on an island in the Atlantic Ocean off the U.S. coast.

better batter
What you might get if Mickey Mantle married Betty Crocker.

bewitches
(bee-WICH-ez) To be along soon. Ex: You go on ahead, I'll bewitches *(be with you)* in a minute.

biennial
(by-EN-ee-al) Purchase without regard to quality. Ex: She'll biennial *(buy any old)* thing so long as it is a bargain.

bier
(BEER) A ghoul's favorite drink.

bigamist
(BIG-a-mist) A denser fog.

bigot
(BIG-ot) Someone who approaches every question with an open mouth and a closed mind.

bigotry
(BIG-a-tree) A tree of larger size.

Big-Blab

bigwig
(BIG-wig) An artificial hairpiece a size too large.

binoculars
(by-NOK-yoo-larz) Parasites. *(pair of sights)*

bird house
Home tweet home.

bird seed
What you plant in your garden to grow canaries.

bison
(BYE-son) What a buffalo says to his male off-spring when he goes off to work.

bitter end
What the puppy did to her tail. Ex: The puppy chased herself until she bitter end. *(bit her end)*

blabbermouth
Someone who shoots straight from the lip. *(hip)*

black eye
The result of a guided muscle.

blackmail
Letters sent from a burned-out post office.

blanket
Something you do to a question on a test when you don't know the answer. *(blank it)*

blastoff
What an astronaut does when he gets angry.

bleached blonde
A woman who dyed by her own hand.

bleachers
That section of a ballpark where the blondes sit.

blind date
Fruit with poor eyesight.

blockhead
A person who gets splinters every time he scratches his head.

blood bank
Where Count Dracula keeps his checking accounts.

blood test
The most important examination in vampire school.

blooming idiots
Half-witted flowers.

Blu-Bo

bluebird
A bird that needs constant cheering up.

boa
A dull snake. *(bore)*

board of education
How some pupils feel about school. *(bored with education)*

boardwalk
An uninteresting stroll. *(bored walk)*

boaster
Someone who, when he opens his mouth, always puts his feats in.

bombard
(bom-BARD) A dreadful poet.

bombshell
An exploding egg.

Boo-Bow

boo-boo
A pair of ghosts.

bookworm
The most educated of insects because it eats up knowledge.

bookworms
Bait a librarian takes along for fishing.

boomerang
What you get by crossing a cannon and a bell.

boot camp
Summer resort for tall shoes.

boring speaker
(1) A person who has nothing to say and says it.
(2) Someone who never makes a long story short.

born loser
Someone who goes through life pushing doors marked "Pull."

borrowed time
Someone else's watch.

borrower
A person who wants to be left alone (*a loan*).

bower
(BOW-er) A dog.

bowling
(1) A sport that is supposed to take you off the streets, but lands you in the alleys. (2) A game in which you build yourself up by knocking things down.

Box-Bran

box lunch
A square meal.

box score
Musical arrangement by Bach. *(Bach's score)*

boyhood
A young male juvenile delinquent.

braggart
Someone who is always letting off esteem *(steam)*.

brainwash
How you clean up a dirty mind.

branch bank
Where money grows on trees.

branding iron
A hot tip.

brass band
A ring that turns green on your finger.

brat
A child at his pest behavior.

brave person
The first one to use the guest towel.

Brazil nut
The wild man who lives at the mouth of the Amazon River.

bread
(1) Sliced food used in some restaurants to keep the insides of sandwiches from blowing away. (2) Raw toast.

bridle path
Aisle the bride walks down.

briefcase
A short lawsuit.

broadcast
A group of plump actors.

broken record
A smash hit.

bronchitis
(brong-KY-tis) A disease found among rodeo riders.

buccaneer
(buck-a-NEER) Highly overpriced corn-on-the-cob.

Buck-Bud

bucking bronco
    A horse that swallowed a dollar.

budget
    What you cannot do to an immovable object.

bulldog
An untruthful canine.

bulldozer
Someone who sleeps through political speeches.

bullfighter
The most truthful person in Spain.

bum steer
An absolutely worthless bull.

bunk bed
Where a liar sleeps.

buoyant
(BOY-unt) A male insect.

burden
(BUR-den) A bird inside. Ex: A burden *(bird in)* the hand is worth two in the bush.

burple
The color of a burp.

bus driver
Someone who is not afraid to tell everyone where to get off.

busybody
A person who belongs to the meddle *(middle)* class.

buttress
(BUT-ris) A female goat.

cacciatore
(kat-cha-TAWR-ee) What American soldiers in the Revolutionary War tried to do. *(catch a Tory)*

cactus
Mother Nature's pincushion.

calcium
(KAL-see-um) What Cal said when he saw 'um.

calories
(KAL-uh-reez) A lot of people can't count calories and have the figures to prove it.

calves
The two animals that follow your every step.

Camelot
(KAM-a-lot) Arabian parking lot. *(camel lot)*

campaign
(kam-PAYN) The worst kid in camp. *(camp pain)*

camphor
(KAM-for) A place one goes for a brief summer vacation. Ex: I went to camphor *(camp for)* two weeks.

Canadian bacon
Money, in Montreal.

candidate
(KAN-di-dayt) A fruit with a sugar coating. *(candied date)*

candlemaker
A person who works only wick ends *(weekends)*.

candy striper
One of Santa's helpers.

cannibal
(KAN-e-bl) A person who is fed up with people.

canoe
(ka-NOO) (1) Like a naughty child, it behaves better when paddled. (2) To question another person. Ex: I can row, canoe *(can you)*?

Canop-Cap

can opener
Key to the washroom.

canopies
(KAN-a-peez) A common item on supermarket shelves. *(can of peas)*

cantaloupe
(Kan-tuh-lohp) (1) What you say when you don't want to run away to be married. *(can't elope)*

(2) What a tired horse says to his rider. *(can't lope)*

canteen
(kan-TEEN) A thirst-aid kit.

cap gun
Pistol worn on the head.

carbuncle
(KAR-bung-kl) An auto collision.

cardinal number
A quantity of birds, the males of which are bright red.

careless pedestrian
(KAYR-lis ped-EST-ree-an) A person who is easily reached by car.

cargo
What gasoline makes an automobile do.

carpet
(1) An animal that enjoys riding in automobiles.
(2) A floor covering that is sold by the yard but worn by the foot.

carrion
(KAR-ee-un) (1) To bring on board. *(carry on)*
(2) To continue a task. (3) To make a disturbance of some kind.

carsickness
Disease contracted by an automobile.

cartoon
A song you sing in an automobile.

cashew
(kash-OO) What you say when you sneeze.

castanet
(kas-ta-NET) To fish without a hook. *(cast a net)*

Cast-Cem

castile
(ka-STEEL) The strongest kind of soap. *(cast steel)*

castor oil
A lubricant for fishing rods.

casualty
(KA-zhoo-uhl-tee) Tea drunk in a relaxed fashion.

caterpillar
A worm in a fur coat.

cat's cradle
Kitten's bassinet.

cattle rustler
A beef thief.

cauliflower
The flower Lassie wears to parties. *(collie flower)*

cauterize
(KAW-ta-ryze) Attract a person's attention. Ex: He cauterize *(caught her eyes)* and she winked back.

cavity
A hole in one.

celery
What you get for working. *(salary)*

cemetery
(SEM-a-ter-ee) A place people are dying to get into.

census
(SEN-sus) There are five: sight, smell, taste, hearing and touch.

center
What one smells with. *(scenter)*

Ceylon
What Christopher Columbus ordered his men to do when they wanted to turn back. *(sail on)*

chaperone
(SHAP-er-ohn) To try different places for the best value or price. *(shop around)*

chargeable
(CHAR-je-bl) What the toreador does. *(charge a bull)*

charging elephant
An elephant who uses his credit card.

Cha-Che

charm school
Where witches learn to cast spells.

chatterbox
(1) Someone who burns the scandal at both ends.
(2) A person vaccinated by a phonograph needle.

cheapskate
A performer on ice who pinches pennies.

Cheerios
Hula hoops for ants.

cheerleaders
The happiest people at a football game.

cheetah
(CHEE-tah) An animal that is not to be trusted.

chestnut
(1) Someone who is crazy about chess. (2) A Raquel Welch fan.

chest of drawers
Where the lungs of artists are found.

chewing gum
Doing it makes you look wriggly *(Wrigley)* all over.

chicken of the sea
A frightened skindiver.

chicken pox
Playgrounds for poultry. *(chicken parks)*

chickens
The only animals you eat before they are born and after they are dead.

childish game
Any game at which you are beaten.

child psychologists
Young people who know how to handle their parents.

Chile
A country where people wear overcoats all year long.

chilipepper
(CHIL-ee-pep-er) Something that is hot and cold at the same time.

chinchilla
(chin-CHIL-ah) An icepack designed for the lower part of the face. *(chin chiller)*

Chin-Chr

Chinese checkers
Customs officials in the Orient.

Chinese spy
(1) A Peiping Tom. (2) A Peking Tom.

chiropractor
(KY-ro-prak-ter) A doctor from the capital of Egypt. *(Cairo practor)*

choke
A funny story.

chop-chop
Two karate blackbelts.

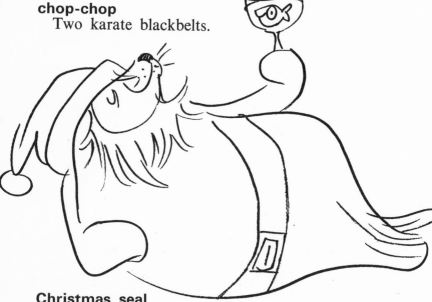

Christmas seal
Santa Claus with flippers.

Christmas shoppers
People who are caught up in the spirit of brotherly shove.

cigarette
A bit of tobacco with a fire at one end and a fool at the other.

Cincinnati
(sin-sin-AT-ee) The wickedest city in the United States.

cinder
(SIN-der) One of the first things to catch your eye when you are traveling next to an open window.

Cinderella
Cinderella was thrown off the team because she ran away from the ball.

circuit
(SUR-kit) A young cat who has been knighted. *(Sir Kit)*

circumnavigate
(sur-kum-NAV-e-gayt) What you say to a knight when you want him to steer the boat. *(Sir, come navigate.)*

city slicker
A raincoat worn only in town.

civil service
Polite treatment one expects in a restaurant.

clam digger
A mussel-bound beachcomber.

classic
A book that everyone praises and nobody reads.

Clau-Clo

claustrophobia
(KLAW-stroh-FOH-bee-a)   An   unreasonable   or
uncontrollable fear of Saint Nick.

cleaners
Depressing place.

clean-living
The life of a sanitation worker.

cleanup
Something nobody notices unless you don't do it.

cliff
(1) A pushover. (2) It isn't always easy to tell the
difference between a real cliff and a bluff.

climate
What you have to do to reach the top of a tree.
(climb it)

clipper ships
Vessels on which the first barbers came to
America.

clock factory
A place where people are paid to make faces.

clocks
Alarming objects.

clockwise
Someone who really knows how to tell time.

close call
Telephone conversation with a next-door neigh-
bor.

closed mind
A person who refuses to take "know" for an answer.

cock-and-bull story
Odd barn yard romance.

cocktail
The back feathers of a rooster.

coconut
Someone who is crazy about hot chocolate. *(cocoa nut)*

C.O.D.
A type of fish brought by the mailman. *(cod)*

Cof-Col

coffee
(KAH-fee) A hot drink that sometimes tastes like mud, especially when it is freshly ground.

coincide
(koh-in-SYDE) What people do when it rains. *(go inside)*

cold cash
Money kept in the freezer compartment of a refrigerator.

cold comfort
A broken electric blanket.

cold cut
A wound inflicted by an icicle.

cold front
What you've got when you stand with your back to the fireplace.

cold war
A snowball fight.

Colo-Com

color
Something that is fast when it doesn't run, and not fast when it does.

colorless
To phone a lady less frequently. *(call her less)*

comedian
A person who knows a good gag when he steals one.

comet
A planet with a hotfoot.

comma
A period with a tail.

commentator
(KAHM-en-tay-ter) An ordinary spud.

committee
(1) A group of the unfit, appointed by the unwilling, to do the unnecessary. (2) A body that keeps minutes and wastes hours.

common sense
Ordinary body odors. *(scents)*

Communist plot
The place where Stalin is buried.

community chest
Where the public heart can be heard beating.

compliment
The applause *(pause)* that refreshes.

Comp-Con

compound sentence
What a person gets if he is convicted of two or more crimes at the same time.

compressed air
A millionaire's oldest son run over by a steam roller. *(compressed heir)*

compromise
An agreement that displeases each side equally.

concave
A hole in the ground frequented by criminals.

conceit
A case of "I" strain.

Concord grape
A fruit defeated in battle. *(conquered grape)*

concourse
(KAHN-kawrs) A class that teaches how to become a successful criminal.

conductor
The musician most likely to get struck by lightning.

Confederate bugler
A rebel rouser.

conference
(KON-fer-ens) A meeting at which people talk about what they should be doing.

confidence
What you start off with before you completely understand the situation.

confirm
(kon-FIRM) A Mafia-run business organization.

Congressional Record
The U.S. Senate's latest disk.

connections
What electricians are always trying to make.

connoisseur
(kon-a-*SUR*) Rather tender. Ex: I rode a horse all day and now I'm connoisseur *(kind of sore)*.

conscience
That small voice that makes you feel even smaller.

contacts
A tax on criminals. *(con tax)*

Contr-Coo

contrite
(kuhn-TRYT) Lack of ability with the written word. Ex: George writes beautifully, but I contrite *(can't write)* a thing.

controversy
(KON-trah-vur-see) A collision between two trains of thought.

convincing talker
Someone who can keep his hands in his pockets while describing a circular staircase.

convulse
(kon-VULS) A dance for prisoners to music by Johann Strauss. *(con waltz)*

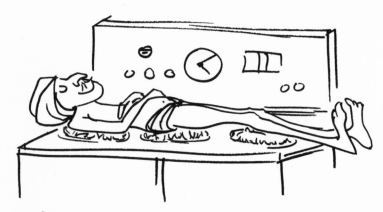

cook
Someone at home on the range.

cookbook
A book with many stirring chapters.

cool person
Someone who can look like an owl, though he has just acted like a jackass.

copycat
The cool guy who runs the Xerox machine.

copyright
To get it down accurately the first time.

coquette
(koh-KET) A popular soft drink.

corn crib
Where old jokes sleep.

corpse
A human been *(being)*.

cosmetics
(koz-MET-iks) Stuff used by young girls to make them look older sooner, and by their mothers to make them look younger longer.

count
A nobleman who knows his arithmetic.

Count Dracula
A big pain in the neck.

counterfeit money
Homemade bread.

counterspy
A store detective.

Cour-Cri

courtly love
A tennis game in which neither player has scored.

coward
A person who, at the slightest sign of danger, thinks with his feet.

cows
Cows do not give milk; you have to take it from them.

crabapple
A grouchy fruit.

crank
Something that makes revolutions.

cream
A liquid that is often whipped on Sundays *(sundaes)*.

crematory
(KREE-ma-taw-ree) To beat someone who supported the British in the Revolutionary War. *(cream a Tory)*

crime reporter
The first with the worst.

crime wave
What you get if you cross the ocean with a thief.

criminal mind
A scheme engine.

criminal record
A stolen phonograph disk that contains a long-playing sentence.

criminal shellfish
A mobster lobster.

croquette
(krow-KET) A romantic lady frog. *(croak-ette)*

crossbow
An angry boyfriend. *(cross beau)*

cross examination
Quiz prepared by an angry teacher.

cross-country skiing
Bad weekend in the mountains.

crow
A bird that never complains without caws *(cause)*.

Crow-Cy

crowbar
Where crows go to drink.

cubic
(KYOO-bik) The language spoken in Cuba.

cuckoo
Someone who prepares food. Ex: We have a cuckoo *(cook who)* makes delicious soup.

cucumber
A drunken vegetable because it is often pickled.

cultured pearl
A gem that has been exposed to the best in the arts and the sciences.

cupid
(KYOO-pid) The little guy who makes a hit with every miss.

curtail
(kur-TAYL) A mutt's end.

cuticle
Charming little icicle.

cutlass
(KUT-las) A wounded young lady.

cyclone
Air in a big rush.

cyclops
Motorcycle policemen. *(cycle cops)*

D.K.
(1) If your teeth have it, see your dentist.
(2) Abbreviation for the most popular words in the English language: Don't Know.

daffodil
A crazy, mixed-up pickle. *(daffy dill)*

dandelion
(1) A dressed-up lion. (2) A fancy line used by a rich fisherman. (3) Pretty good fibbing.

dandruff
A chip off the old block.

Dark Ages
Knight time.

dashing personality
A well-known track and field athlete.

data
What a baby computer calls its father.

date
(1) A fruit found on calendars. (2) Eating dates is time consuming.

Dat-Dec

dateline
A phony story told during a boy-girl meeting.

daze
More than one twenty-four hour period. *(days)*

dead center
A stuffed nose.

dead giveaway
A cancelled quiz show.

dead ringer
(1) A corpse leaning against a doorbell. (2) A deceased Avon lady. (3) A broken alarm clock.

death
Patrick Henry's second choice.

debate
What lures the fish.

deceit
(di-SEET) (1) A piece of furniture on which one sits. (2) The back part of a pair of jeans.

decentralize
(dee-SEN-truh-lyze) The middle eyes of a five-eyed monster.

declare
Cloudless. Ex: I gazed into declare *(the clear)* blue skies.

decomposes
(dee-kum-POHZ-ez) What a dead composer does.

decoration
A speech made while standing on a ship. *(deck oration)*

deduce
(dee-DOOS) The lowest card in the deck. *(the deuce)*

deer
Wealthy animal species known for its bucks.

defeat
What you walk on.

defeated politician
Like the earth—flattened at the polls.

deficiency
(di-FISH-en-see) The creatures that live in the ocean.

Defo-Den

Defoe
(di-FOH) The enemy author. (Daniel Defoe, 1659?–1731)

degraded
How you feel when you have earned a low mark.

delighted
What happens to a firefly if it backs into a fan.

denial
The main river of Egypt. *(the Nile)*

denominator
The person who names a candidate.

denounce
(de-NOWNS) Not verbs or adjectives. *(the nouns)*

dentist
(1) A person who gets paid for boring you. (2) The biggest Yank of them all. (3) Someone who can give you the drill of your life.

dentist's office
A filling station.

deodorant
(de-OH-der-unt) The other close female relative.
Ex: Not this aunt, deodorant *(the other aunt)*.

depend
Not the shallow part of the pool—the other end.
(deep end)

depress
A printing machine that prints only sad news.

depth
Height upside down.

descent
(de-SENT) (1) A small coin. (2) An odor.

despair
The extra tire.

detour
(DEE-toor) A road where no turn is left un-stoned.

devise
(dee-VYZE) Persons of considerable intelligence.
Ex: A word to devise *(the wise)* should be sufficient.

devote
(duh-VOHT) What an office seeker desires more than anything else.

Di-Dim

dialogue
(DYE-a-log) To perish in utter misery. Ex: Insult the queen and you dialogue *(die like)* a dog!

diamond
There is nothing harder than a diamond, except paying for it.

diamond cutter
The person who mows the grass on a baseball field.

diamond in the rough
A baseball field still under construction.

dictionary
(1) A book in which you can always find health, wealth, and happiness. (2) A guide to the correct spelling of words, provided you know how to spell them in the first place. (3) The one place where Friday comes before Thursday.

diet
A triumph of mind over platter.

dieter
(1) A wishful shrinker *(thinker)*. (2) A person who hopes to mend his weighs *(ways)*.

digital computer
(DIJ-i-tl kom-PYOO-ter) Someone who counts on his fingers.

dimension
(di-MEN-shun) A polite remark. Ex: "Thank you." "Dimension *(don't mention)* it."

dimple

A pimple going the other way.

diploma

(di-PLOH-mah) The man who fixes the leaks in water pipes. *(the plumber)*

diplomacy

(di-PLOH-mah-see) The art of saying something when you have nothing to say, and of saying nothing when you have something to say.

diplomat

(DIP-luh-mat) (1) A person who can bring home the bacon without spilling the beans. (2) Someone who can tell you to go to hell with such tact, you actually look forward to the trip.

dirt

Mud with the juice squeezed out.

Dirt-Dis

dirty double crosser
A person who sails to Europe and back without washing.

dirty liar
A musical instrument that needs a good cleaning. *(dirty lyre)*

dirty two-timers
A pair of stopwatches in the mud.

disease
(di-ZEEZ) Those areas of the earth covered with water. *(the seas)*

disguise
The upper regions of the atmosphere. *(the skies)*

disk jockey
A person in show business who lives on spins and needles.

distinct
How one can tell the difference between skunks and other animals.

divine
What the grapes grow on. *(the vine)*

division
The sense of sight. *(the vision)*

Doberman pinscher
The freshest fellow in the town of Doberman.

doctor
(1) Someone who practices medicine but charges as if he knew. (2) A person with inside information.

dog
An animal that should never be allowed near a flea circus, because he might walk off with the show.

dog catcher
A Spot remover.

dog house
A mutt hut.

dog kennel
A barking lot.

dogma
(DOG-mah) A mother dog.

dogmatic
(dog-MAT-ik) The kind of gun carried by German shepherds.

dog pound
A used cur *(car)* lot.

dogwood
A tree distinguished by its bark.

double checks
A pair from Czechoslovakia.

double crosser
Someone with a great sense of two-timing.

double-decker bed
A lot of bunk.

double-header
A two-headed monster.

double stitch
A sew-and-sew.

doublet
  (DUB-let) To increase by twice the amount.
  (double it)

double take
  What a pair of shoplifters make off with.

double-talk
  A schizophrenic parrot.

doughnut
  (1) A person just wild about money. (2) A strong
  warning. Ex: Doughnut *(do not)* open the door!

down in the mouth
  What you might get if you eat a duck.

dragon
  Move in a sluggish way. Ex: Time sure is dragon
  (dragging) without you.

Dra-Dri

dragon milk
Milk from a short-legged cow.

draw
The result of a struggle between a dentist and his patient.

dreadful actor
An abominable showman.

dreamer
A man who has both feet planted firmly in the clouds.

driblet
What you do with a basketball. *(dribble it)*

drill sergeant
An army dentist.

dry dock
A thirsty physician.

duck
A bird that walks as though it had been riding on a horse all day.

duet
Accomplish a task. Ex: There's a right and a wrong way to duet *(do it)*.

dumbwaiter
Someone who can't get your order right.

duty
(1) Something we look forward to with distaste, do with reluctance, and boast about forever after.
(2) What we expect from others.

dynamite
A boom stick.

earth
A minor planet with major problems.

earthquake
Mother Nature doing the twist.

eavesdrop
(EEVZ-drop) What happens when the roof falls in.

echo
What always talks back no matter who you are.

eclipse
(e-KLIPS) What a gardener does to a hedge. *(he clips)*

economy
(e-KON-uh-mee) Large size in soap flakes, but small size in automobiles.

ecstasy
(EK-stuh-see) What is on view in a hen house. *(eggs to see)*

egg
A peculiar object; it is not beaten unless it is good.

eggplant
A factory for the manufacture of eggs.

Egg White
Snow White's brother.

egomaniac
(EE-go-MAYN-ee-ak) A person of low taste, more interested in himself than in me.

egotist
(EE-guh-tist) Someone who is usually in me-deep conversation.

Eiffel Tower
(EYE-fel TOW-er) An erector set that made good.

El-Ele

elastic
(uh-LAS-tik) The sound made by a watch just before it stops. *(the last tick)*

elections
Events held to find out if the opinion polls were right.

electric fan
Someone who gets a big charge out of electricity.

electrician
(e-lek-TRISH-an) A person who wires for money.

elephants
The most modest of animals. They always bathe with their trunks on.

elephant stew
The recipe is simple. Just make the elephant wait for two hours, and he'll stew!

elevator operator
A person who is always ready to give others a lift.

eliminate
(uh-LIM-uh-nayt) A cold, refreshing drink made from lemons and sugar. *(a lemonade)*

emergency
(uh-MER-jen-see) What you might say to a groundhog on February 2. *(emerge and see)*

emigrate
(EM-uh-grayt) A smug, egotistical expression. Ex: Emigrate *(I'm a great)* fellow, don't you agree?

Emission Impossible
Making cars pollution-free this year.

emote
(e-MOHT) A small body of water surrounding a castle. *(a moat)*

enchanted banana
A slipping *(sleeping)* beauty.

endeavor
(en-DEV-er) A very long time. Ex: I'll be your friend for ever endeavor *(and ever)*.

endless speech
Like a wheel—the longer the spoke, the greater the tire.

endorse
(en-DAWRS) The best place to be when it is raining. *(indoors)*

Endo-Ent

endow
(en-DOW) The means by which you intend to accomplish a goal. Ex: Endow *(and how)* do you intend to get us out of this mess?

energy crisis
When it becomes too hard to fuel *(fool)* all of the people all of the time.

engineers
What engines hear with.

English Channel
A British television station.

enlist
(en-LIST) N, n, n, n, n, n, n, n, n, n, n, n, etc.

enterprise
(EN-ter-pryze) An award won by someone at the door.

entrance
(EN-truhns) Be in a deep hypnotic state. *(in trance)*

enunciate
(uh-NUNS-ee-ayt) What gave the cannibal queen an upset stomach. *(a nun she ate)*

epitome
(uh-PIT-uh-mee) Feel dreadfully ill. Ex: I felt sick to epitome *(the pit of my)* stomach when I saw her.

erase
A contest to determine who is the swiftest. *(a race)*

Erie Canal
A body of water haunted by ghosts.

erosion
(e-ROH-zhun) The Great Terrain *(train)* Robbery.

escalator
Inquire at some future time. Ex: Escalator *(ask her later)*, she is too busy to talk now.

eschew
(es-CHOO) The sound made by someone with a cold.

Eskimos
(ES-ki-mohz) God's frozen people.

Eskimo shoes
Mush puppies.

Et-Ev

Etc.
(et-SET-er-a) An abbreviation used to make people believe you know more than you do.

Ether Bunny
(EETH-er BUN-ee) An anaesthetized rabbit.

ethereal
(e-THEER-ee-al) A common breakfast food. *(a cereal)*

etiquette
(ET-i-ket) The difference between table manners and stable manners.

Euclid
(YOO-klid) A strong expression of admiration. Ex: I love my wife—but oh, Euclid *(you kid)*!

eureka
(YOO-ree-kah) A sophisticated way of saying, "You stink!" *(you reek)*

Europe
(YOOR-up) To be out of bed and awake. Ex: I see Europe *(you're up)* early today, for a change.

European
Insult. Ex: European (You're a pain) in the neck.

evaporated milk
The kind of milk preferred by the invisible man.

Everest
The laziest mountain in the world.

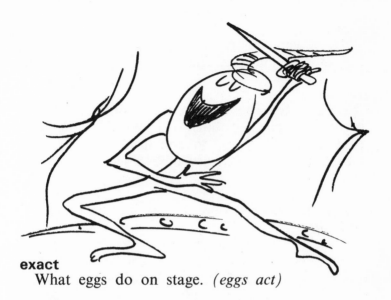

exact
What eggs do on stage. *(eggs act)*

examine
To have eggs plus ham plus something else. Ex: Waiter, may I please have examine *(eggs, ham and)* toast?

excel
(ek-SEL) The market price for eggs. Ex. Excel *(eggs sell)* for 90 cents per dozen these days.

excess fat
Not the result of the minutes you put in at the dinner table, but the seconds.

exchequer
(eks-CHEK-er) A retired supermarket clerk. *(ex-checker)*

exclamation point
(ek-skla-MAY-shun poynt) A period blowing its top.

Exe-Exp

executive
(eg-ZEK-yoo-tiv) A person who gets someone else to do a job he dislikes.

exercise
(EKS-er-syze) The only exercise some people get is to: (1) pile up bills; (2) wrestle with their conscience; (3) jump to conclusions; (4) stretch the truth; or (5) run out of excuses.

exit
What the teacher does to an incorrect answer. *("X" it)*

experience
(1) What you have left after you have lost everything else. (2) The wonderful knowledge that enables you to recognize a mistake after you have made it.

expert
An expert is a person who skillfully avoids the small errors only to sweep on to the really big one.

expertise
(eks-per-TEEZ) The most popular girl in school. *(expert tease)*

explain
Eggs cooked without any trimmings. *(eggs plain)*

express
A bankrupt printing firm. *(ex-press)*

exterminator
(ek-STUR-mi-nayt-er) A hired killer who does not go to jail.

extreme
(eks-TREEM) A dried up river bed. *(ex-stream)*

eye doctor
An Iris-man. *(Irishman)*

eyesore
(EYE-saw) An emphatic expression. Ex: Eyesore *(I sure)* do like you!

face lift
An elevator that takes only part of you up.

failure
A person who generally takes the path of least persistence.

falling arches
Samson was killed by them.

falsehood
A person who pretends to be a gangster.

false teeth
(1) Like the stars, they come out at night. (2) Many a true word is spoken through false teeth.

falsify
(FAWL-se-fye) Cause something to drop to the ground. Ex: When I put a book on my head, it falsify *(falls if I)* move.

family swimming pool
A small body of water completely surrounded by other people's children.

famous composer
A person of note.

fanatic
(fa-NAT-ik) A person who is enthusiastic about something in which you are not at all interested.

fancy restaurant
A place where you may order something superior for your interior.

fanfare
An exhibition of fans. *(fan fair)*

fan magazine
A magazine to keep you cool in hot weather.

Far-Fe

farmer
(1) A person outstanding in his field. (2) Someone who works from daybreak to backbreak.

fascinate
(FAS-e-nayt) A number of buttons you can close. Ex: My coat has ten buttons, but I can only fascinate *(fasten eight)*.

fastidious
(fa-STID-ee-us) A monster who is quick and hideous.

fat
The penalty for exceeding the feed limit.

fat cashiers
Chubby checkers.

fat cat
A flabby tabby.

fat chance
Slim chance.

fatso
(FAT-soh) A thin person who has gone to waist.

faucet
(FAW-set) Use brute strength. Ex: The door is stuck; don't faucet *(force it)*.

feather bed
Where feathers sleep.

feed store
The only place where you can get a chicken dinner for 10 cents.

felon
(FEL-uhn) Drop from a height. Ex: The tree felon *(fell on)* his head.

fence
The difference between one yard and two yards.

fencing lessons
Instructions on how to repair fences.

ferryboat
Something that makes every passenger cross.

fewer
(FYOO-er) A question of fact. Ex: Fewer *(if you were)* a real friend, you would lend me your bicycle.

Fi-Fir

fickle pickle
A dill that keeps changing its mind.

fiddler crab
A rather grouchy violinist.

fiddlesticks
What you play violins with.

figurehead
(FIG-yer-hed) Mathematical genius.

file
A place where everything is arranged alphabetically and lost systematically.

filibuster
(FIL-uh-bus-ter) A cowboy who breaks in young mares. *(filly buster)*

filly
A young horse from Pennsylvania. *(Philly)*

finance
(fy-NANS) Elegant insects. *(fine ants)*

firecracker
A hot cookie.

firefly
An insect that does well in school because it is so bright.

fireman
Someone who ought to go to blazes.

fireside
The warmest part of the house.

firing line
A dangerous geometric figure.

first aid kit
A cat that works for the Red Cross.

fish
An animal that manages to go on vacation at the same time as most fishermen.

fisherman
(1) A sportsman who sometimes catches a big fish by patience, sometimes by luck, but most often by the tale. (2) A person who often drops the fish a line, but seldom hears from them. (3) A jerk at one end of the line waiting for a jerk at the other end.

fishhook
A town in northern New Jersey, so named because it is the end of the line.

Fish-Fiv

fishing tackle
A football player with rod and reel.

fission
(FISH-un) Where atomic scientists go when they have time off.

fission chips
(FISH-un chips) An atomic scientist's favorite food.

five-cent cucumber
A nickel pickle.

fixture
(FIKS-cher) Repaired something of yours. Ex: The mechanic fixture *(fixed your)* automobile today.

fjord
(FYORD) A famous make of Norwegian automobile.

flashlight
A case in which to carry dead batteries.

flat face
The result of keeping your nose to the grindstone.

flattery
(FLAT-e-ree) Soft soap, composed of 90 per cent lye *(lie)*.

flaw
The part of the room opposite the ceiling. *(floor)*

fleabag
What you carry fleas in.

flea market
Where fleas do their shopping.

fleece
Little insects that live on sheep and cause itching and scratching. *(fleas)*

flies
(1) Insects that are excellent mathematicians: they add misery, subtract pleasure, divide attention and multiply rapidly. (2) Some people shoo them; others just let them run around barefoot.

Fli-Fly

flirting
Wishful winking.

flood
A river that has grown too big for its bridges *(britches)*.

flowers
Lazy forms of plant life. They are often found in beds.

fly-by-night
An airplane trip after dark.

fly casting
Lining up flies for parts in a movie or play.

flying saucer
One dish that is truly out of this world.

flying tackle
Bird bait.

flypaper
(1) Blueprint for an airplane. (2) The best material for making kites. (3) A newspaper read by insects.

fodder
(FAHD-er) A male parent.

folder
Pertaining to senior citizens. Ex: We all should have more respect folder *(for older)* people.

folk-rock
Object used to stone people.

food
All a matter of taste.

foolhardy
A healthy idiot.

fools
Fools, like fish, would not get into trouble if they kept their mouths shut and didn't fall for any old line.

football
A brown leather object fought over by 22 men.

football coach
A vehicle used to transport sports equipment.

Foot-Fou

footnotes
Music played by a shoehorn.

forays
A, A, A, A.

foreground
A golf course.

foreheads
What a pair of Siamese twins have. *(4 heads)*

forfeit
(FOR-fit) What dogs, cats, horses and most other animals walk on. *(four feet)*

forger
(FAWR-jer) Someone who is always ready to write a wrong.

fortress
A female fort.

fortune
Music to everyone's ears.

forum
(FOR-um) (1) Two-um plus two-um. (2) Opposite of against-um.

foul ball
Where chickens go to dance.

foul language
What you hear if you pass near the chicken coop.

foul shot
   A chicken, duck, or turkey struck by a bullet.

four quarters
   What the moon is worth.

four seasons
   Salt, pepper, mustard, and vinegar.

francs
   French hot dogs. *(franks)*

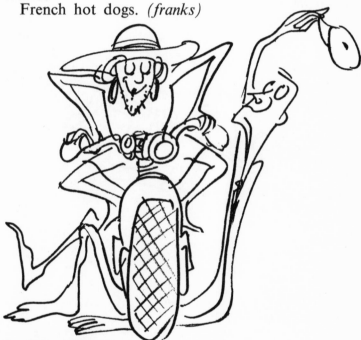

freak accident
   What happened, for example, when the bearded
   lady ran into the rubber man.

freckles
   A suntan that hasn't gotten it all together.

Free-Fres

free agent
A spy who didn't get caught.

free-lance
A knight who doesn't charge for his services.

free speech
When you can use someone else's phone.

French bread
Money in France.

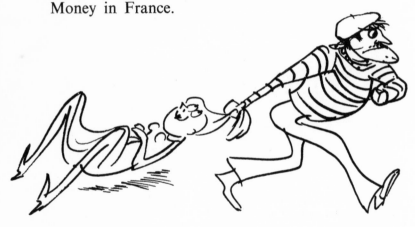

French heel
Low character from Paris.

French toast
"Cheers" in French.

fresh fish
Sea creatures with cheeky ways.

fresh peanuts
Some peanuts are so fresh, they are positively insulting.

friar
(FRY-er) A religious young chicken.

Friday
The best day of the week for frying.

friend
One who always excuses you when you have made a fool of yourself.

frog
An animal that croaks all the time but means it only once.

frontiersmen
(front-EERS-men) People with ears on the front of their faces rather than to the sides.

fullback
A fullback is equal to four quarterbacks.

fungus
(FUNG-us) A chap named Gus who is a lot of laughs.

furor
(FYOO-ror) The leader of Nazi Germany.

game fowl
Poultry that's ready for anything.

game warden
Official who supervises play equipment.

garbage dump
The community scenter.

garbage men
(1) They have the saddest job, because they are down in the dumps so much. (2) They are truthful, because they smell it like it is.

gardeners
Professional grafters.

garden hose
Socks worn while you work in the garden.

gardening
Someone's effort to improve his lot.

garden plot
A story about plants.

garlic
(GAHR-lik) Vegetable which is excellent for avoiding cold germs. Eat enough of it and people with colds will stay far away from you. Of course, so will other people.

garter snake
A perfectly harmless reptile, but it has been known to snap on occasion.

gatekeeper
A person who fails to return the gates you lend him.

genealogy
(jee-nee-OL-a-jee) The study of genies.

General Electric
A high army officer noted for his shocking personality.

generally
The head of the Confederate Army in the Civil War. *(General Lee)*

Gen-Gh

gentleman
Someone who can keep his shirt on while getting something off his chest.

Gentlemen of the Press
Polite tailors.

geologist
(jee-OL-uh-jist) (1) Fault finder. (2) Person with rocks on his mind.

geometry
(jee-OM-uh-tree) What the acorn said with pride after it had grown into an oak. *(Gee, I'm a tree.)*

George Washington Bridge
The first American President's dentures.

germ
A tiny, one-celled creature with the incredible ability to multiply by division.

gestation
(JES-tay-shun) Where you normally get off. Ex: We just passed gestation *(your station)*.

geyser
(GYE-zer) Mother Nature steamed up about something.

ghetto
(GET-oh) Depart immediately. Ex: Ghetto *(Get a-)* way from me, you monster, you!

ghost
A shadow of its former self.

ghost writer
A spooksman.

gibbon
(GIB-on) To treat someone in a particular way. Ex: I wish you would stop gibbon *(giving)* me such a hard time.

gingerbread house
A place you can call "home sweet home" and really mean it.

giraffe
The highest form of animal life.

Gir-Go

girdle
(1) A device used to keep an unfortunate condition from spreading. (2) Proof that figures can lie.

girlhood
A young female juvenile delinquent.

gladiator
(GLAD-ee-ay-ter) What the cannibal was, after lunching on the lady explorer. *(glad he ate her)*

glasswork
What a window does for a living.

gnu
(NOO) (1) Opposite of old. Ex: What's gnu *(new)*, Pussycat? (2) Past tense of to know. Ex: I gnu *(knew)* him a long time ago. (3) Information about events. Ex: There are two kinds of gnus *(news)*: good gnus and bad gnus.

goat
An animal that has the bad habit of butting in.

goblet
(1) A small sailor. (2) A young turkey.

Golden Gate Bridge
The car-spangled spanner.

goldfish
Wet pet.

gold soup
Soup made with 14 carrots *(carats)*.

golf
(1) A game in which a ball one and a half inches in diameter is placed on a ball some 8,000 miles in diameter. The object is to hit the small ball and not the larger one. (2) Used to be called a rich man's game, but now there are millions of poor players.

golf ball
(1) A small round object which remains on the tee while a perspiring citizen fans it vigorously with a large club. (2) A golf ball is a golf ball no matter how you slice it. (3) Where golfers go to dance.

golf socks
Hose with 18 holes in them.

Goliath
(goh-LYE-eth) Recline. Ex: Why don't you Goliath *(go lie)* down, you look tired.

Goo-Goos

good-bye
A bargain. *(good buy)*

good manners
Making your company feel at home, even though you wish they were.

good talkers
People who can keep their hands in their pockets while they describe the fish that got away.

goose
A bird that grows down as it grows up.

goose pimples
What a goose gets from eating too much chocolate.

gorilla
(1) An animal you wouldn't want to monkey around with. (2) Food prepared by gentle heating. Ex: Mother, may I please have a gorilla *(grilled)* cheese sandwich?

gossip
(GAH-sip) (1) A person who will never tell a lie if the truth will do more damage.

gossip columnist
One who writes another's wrongs.

goulash
(GOO-lahsh) What a ghoul wears during rain or snow.

government bureau
Where the taxpayer's shirt is kept.

graham cracker
A metric cookie. *(gram cracker)*

Grand Canyon
Hole of fame.

grand jury
A jury which finds everyone innocent.

granite
(GRAN-it) (1) To agree to do something. Ex: Make a wish and I'll granite *(grant it)*. (2) Fail to properly appreciate someone. Ex: I may only be a stone cutter's daughter, but please don't you take me for granite *(granted)*!

Gra-Gro

grape
A fruit that seldom gets lonely because it comes in bunches.

grass
What grows by the yard and dies by the foot.

grateful
How a fireplace feels when it is filled with logs.

gravedigger
A very down-to-earth guy.

gravely
How an undertaker speaks.

Great Plains
The 747's.

Greece
Where the first doughnuts were fried. *(grease)*

greedy person
A human gimme-pig *(guinea pig)*.

gross ignorance
144 times worse than ordinary ignorance.

grouch
One who, when opportunity knocks, complains about the noise.

ground beef
A cow sitting on the grass.

groundhog
Sausage.

gruesome
(GROO-sum) Increase in size. Ex: Since I was measured, I gruesome *(grew some)*.

guerilla warfare
Monkeys throwing coconuts at each other.

guillotine
(gil-uh-TEEN) A French chopping *(shopping)* center.

gullet
Small seagull.

gunboat
A boat used in shooting rapids.

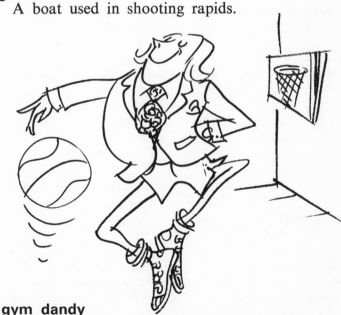

gym dandy
An athlete who wears shirt and tie during a ball game.

H-Ha

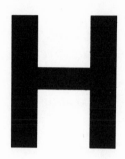

hacienda
(hah-see-EN-da) The conclusion. Ex: Hacienda *(that's the end of)* my story.

hackneyed
To have legs like a taxi cab. *(hack-kneed)*

haddock
(HAD-uk) A dull, throbbing pain in the head often relieved by aspirin. *(headache)*

haggle
A little crone.

hair
A hair on the head is worth two in the brush.

half a loaf
A short vacation.

halfback
What you get in change from a dollar when you spend fifty cents.

half gainer
Swimmer who diets part of the time.

half wit
Someone who spends half his time being funny.

halibut
For no good reason. Ex: We went to the game just for the halibut *(hell of it)*.

halo
(HAY-loh) What one angel says to another angel. *(hello)*

handkerchief
(1) The loss of an expensive handkerchief can be an awful blow. (2) Cold storage.

handsome
Pass something along. Ex: Please handsome *(hand some)* pizza to me.

hand-to-mouth
A yawn.

Hap-Hat

happiness
Happiness is like potato salad: share it with others and you can have a picnic.

happy medium
A good-natured spiritualist.

hard-boiled eggs
Eggs laid by tough chickens.

hard butter
An angry goat.

hard drink
Ice cubes.

hari-kari
(HAR-ee KAR-ee) A wig transported from one place to another.

harmonica
(har-MON-ika) Referring to a woman's name. Ex: Harmonica *(her moniker)* is Typhoid Mary.

harmonious
(hahr-MOH-nee-us) Where we keep our funds. Ex: Harmonious *(our money is)* in the piggy bank.

harp
(1) A piano in the nude. (2) A giant egg slicer.

hasty pudding
Instant dessert.

hatchet
(HACH-it) What a hen does with an egg.

hat rack
Torture instrument for headgear.

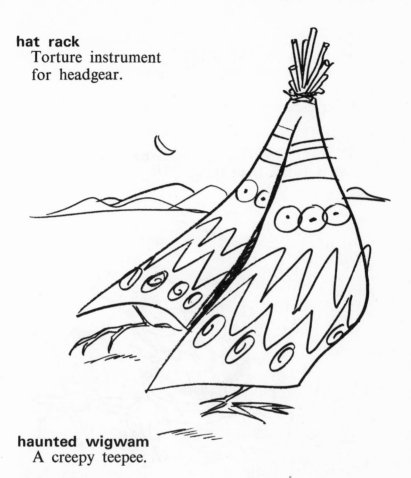

haunted wigwam
A creepy teepee.

haunting melody
A popular tune on the Ghost-to-Ghost network.

hay fever
Flower power.

head cold
Like taking a vote: sometimes the eyes *(ayes)* have it, and sometimes the nose *(no's)*.

Head-Hel

head hunter
The person to see if you have lost your head.

heavy date
A fat escort.

heifer
(HEF-er) Less than full size. Ex: Heifer *(half a)* loaf is better than none.

helium
(HEE-lee-um) What a medicine man tries to do. *(heal 'um)*

hence
Egg-laying chickens.

hermit
What a girl uses when she plays baseball. *(her mitt)*

heroes
What a gentleman does when he is seated in a boat with a lady. *(he rows)*

hero sandwich
What brave soldiers eat.

Hershey bar
Where all the nuts hang out.

hiccup
(HIK-up) A drinking vessel used by country yokels. *(hick cup)*

Hickory dickory dock
A country physician who argues a lot.

high chair
A friendly greeting to a piece of furniture. *(Hi, chair!)*

high noon
Midday on Mt. Everest.

high-school marriage
A teensters' *(teamsters)* union.

high scream
A favorite frozen dessert of ghosts, vampires, ghouls, etc. *(ice cream)*

Hig-Ho

high spirits
(1) What you say when you meet a group of ghosts. *(Hi, spirits!)* (2) Ghosts that haunt skyscrapers.

hillbilly
A goat that prefers mountainous country.

historians
(hi-STAWR-ee-anz) People who won't let bygones be bygones.

history
One man's explanation for what happened. Ex: That's history *(his story)*, but I don't believe a word of it.

hit-and-run
A traffic violation allowed in baseball.

hit song
A tune that stops being popular by the time you learn the words.

hobby-horse
An animal that enjoys collecting stamps or coins.

hobo
A road's *(Rhodes)* scholar.

hockey player
A disk jockey.

hog raiser
A person who makes his living by the pen.

hog wash
Where pigs do their laundry.

hole in one
A cavity.

hollow
An empty greeting.

Hollywood
An evergreen shrub with shiny, sharp-pointed leaves and bright red berries. Ex: Evergreens won't grow here, but Hollywood *(holly would)*.

holy smoke!
Fire in a place of worship.

"Home on the Range"
The teapot's favorite song.

Home-Hor

Homer
(1) A famous Greek who, some say, invented the game of baseball. (2) The guy who made Babe Ruth famous.

hominy
(HOM-in-ee) An unknown number. Ex: Hominy *(how many)* times do I have to tell you to cut that out!

hootenanny
(hoo-ten-AN-ee) What you get if you cross a goat with an owl.

horizon
(huh-RYE-zun) To direct one's attention. Ex: She has horizon *(her eyes on)* me.

horrible example
A very difficult problem in mathematics.

horse
(1) A six-legged animal. It has forelegs in front and two legs behind. (2) An animal that cannot say yes, only nay *(neigh)*.

horse and buggy
Description of an odd person who has laryngitis. *(hoarse and buggy)*

horse doctor
A physician with a sore throat.

horsehair
The presence of someone. Ex: Well, look horsehair *(who's here)*!

horsehide
What helps keep a horse from falling apart.

horseman
A person who is half horse and half man.

horse sense
A quality found most often in persons with a stable mind.

hospital
(1) A place where people who are run down wind up. (2) Where they wake you up to give you a sleeping pill.

hot chocolate
Stolen candy.

hot dog
(1) A mutt wanted by the dog catcher. (2) A long meat roll that feeds the hand that bites it.

Hote-How

hotel
A place where you pay good dollars for poor quarters.

hotline
A telephone in a house with teenagers.

hot rod
A branding iron.

hourglass
What we drink out of. *(our glass)*

housemother
The question to ask about your female parent's health. *(how's mother?)*

House of Correction
(1) The place where teachers go over their pupils' tests. (2) The home of a proofreader.

howling success
(1) A hit show starring dogs. (2) A dog that has won first place in a barking contest.

hula dancer
A shake in the grass.

human body
A living thing so sensitive that if you pat it on the back, its head swells.

human dynamo
A person who charges everything.

humbug
An insect that wants to sing but just doesn't know the words.

humiliate
(hyoo-MIL-ee-ayt) What you might ask a cannibal if you suspected he ate someone called Millie. *(You Millie ate?)*

Humphrey
A suitable name for anyone without humps. *(hump-free)*

Humpty Dumpty
A camel that won't let you ride him.

hunger
What the posse did to the lady rustler. *(hung her)*

hypodermic needle
(HY-poh-DER-mik NEED-l) A sick shooter.

I-Ig

ice
Skid stuff.

ice cream
Yell at the top of your voice. *(I scream)*

ice cream parlour
Fountain of youth.

ice skates
Learning how to stand on them takes several sittings.

icicle
An eavesdropper.

icy sidewalk
An icy sidewalk is like music, if you don't see sharp *(C♯)*, you'll be flat *(B♭)*.

ideal
What you say to a card sharp. *(I deal)*

igloo
What keeps stamps attached to envelopes. *(glue)*

ignorance
(IG-nohr-uns) When you don't know something —and somebody finds it out.

iguana
(ig-WAH-nah) Referring to a desire. Ex: Iguana *(I want to)* hold your hand.

illegal
A sick bird. *(ill eagle)*

impassable
(im-PAS-uh-bl) A wet football.

impeccable
(im-PEK-uh-bl) Something chickens can't eat.

Inca
What you put into your pen in order to write. *(ink)*

Inc-Incr

inchworms
(1) Insects that are worried about what will happen when everything goes metric. (2) It takes 12 of them to make a foot.

incite
(in-SYTE) Where you go when the weather is bad. *(inside)*

income
Enter into. Ex: I opened the door and income the cat.

incongruous
(in-KON-groo-us) Where the laws are made in the United States. *(in Congress)*

increases
(in-KREES-ez) A garment that can use a pressing.

independent
(in-duh-PEN-dunt) Souvenir of the Indianapolis 500. *(Indy pennant)*

index
How playing cards come. *(in decks)*

India
A place where you can say "Holy Cow" and people know what you are talking about.

Indian club
Social organization for people from India.

Indian reservation
The home of the brave.

indigestion
The failure to adjust a square meal to a round stomach.

indistinct
(in-dis-TINGT) Where you put the dirty dishes. *(in the sink)*

infancy
(IN-fan-see) The age of change.

infantry
What babies grow on. *(infant tree)*

infer
(in-FER) What will certainly happen to you. Ex: You're infer *(in for)* big trouble unless you straighten out.

Infl-Ins

inflation
(1) A method of cutting money in half without damaging the paper. (2) A drop in the buck *(bucket)*.

information
How military planes fly. *(in formation)*

ingenious
(in-JEEN-yus) Where a great brain is found.

ingest
(in-JEST) All in fun.

inkling
(INK-ling) A tiny fountain pen.

innocence
(IN-noh-sens) By no conceivable stretch of the imagination. *(in no sense)*

innuendo
(in-yoo-EN-doh) In your window. Ex: Open the curtain and let the light shine innuendo.

insane blackbird
A raven *(raving)* maniac.

insinuate
(in-SIN-yoo-ayt) To have sinned while having a meal.

insulate
(IN-suh-layt) What you are when the school bus doesn't come. *(in so late)*

insurance
What you pay now so when you're dead you'll have nothing to worry about.

insurance policy
Something that, if you get hit on the head, pays a lump sum.

intelligence
A quality clearly shown by anyone who agrees with you.

intelligent
Some people are so intelligent they can speak on any subject. Others don't need a subject.

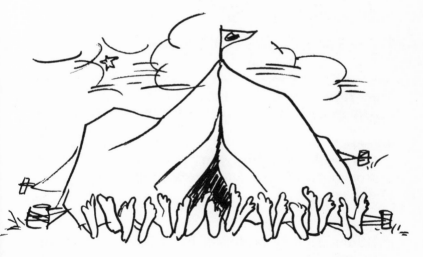

intense
(in-TENS) Where scouts sleep on a camping trip. *(in tents)*

Io-It

I.O.U.
A paper wait *(weight)*.

Iron Age
The period just before the Permanent Press Era.

isolate
(EYE-suh-layt) Why you were not on time. Ex: Isolate *(I was so late)* because the alarm clock did not go off.

isthmus
(IS-muhs) Very probably. Ex: Isthmus *(this must)* be the place.

itch
What happens to your nose whenever both your hands are full.

jackass
(JAK-as) An animal that is popular because it gives kicks to so many people.

jack-in-the-box
An open and shut case.

Jamaica
Did you get. Ex: Jamaica *(did you make a)* good grade in school today?

janitor
(1) A floor flusher. (2) A man who uses sweeping gestures.

jargon
(JAR-gun) A missing container. *(jar gone)*

jasmine
(JAZ-min) A professional musician. *(jazzman)*

jaywalker
A dumb bird with a short life.

jaywalking
A form of exercise that often leads to that run-down feeling.

Je-Jo

jeep
  A vehicle which is uncomfortable to ride. In fact, seven days in a jeep makes one weak *(week)*.

jeers
  A shout of encouragement. Ex: Three jeers *(cheers)* for the home team!

jet-setter
  A fast-flying dog.

jitterbug
  (JIT-er-bug) A nervous insect.

Joan of Arc
  Noah's wife, some say.

joke
  Probably the oldest joke on record is when Eve asked Adam, "Do you love me?" and he replied, "Who else?"

Jonah
> The strongest man in the Bible. Even a whale could not keep him down.

jugular vein
> (JUG-yuh-ler vayn) Someone who thinks he is great just because he can keep 5 plates in the air at the same time. *(juggler vain)*

juicy
> Did you observe? Ex: Juicy *(did you see)* what I just saw?

jungle-gym
> Tarzan's brother. *(Jungle Jim)*

junk
> Something you save for years and then throw away just before you need it.

junkyard
> Where Chinese boats are stored.

jurisdiction
> Words that juries use.

justice
> (1) Only for this occasion. Ex: Justice *(just this)* once, do it my way. (2) As expected. Ex: Justice *(just as)* I thought; you're still in bed.

juvenile delinquent
> (1) A young person who prefers vice to advice. (2) A minor who is a major problem.

K.P.
A term used in the military meaning to "keep peeling."

kangaroo
A pogo stick with a pouch.

karate school
Chop-house.

kernel
The leader of the popcorn brigade. *(colonel)*

ketchup
What the last runner in a race would like to do. *(catch up)*

khaki
(KA-kee) A small metal object which must be inserted into the dashboard to start up the automobile. *(car key)*

kidnap
What a small child often does after lunch.

kilocycle
Vicious bike. *(killer cycle)*

kindergarten teacher
Someone who knows how to make the little things count.

kindred
(KIN-dred) An abnormal fear of relatives. *(kin dread)*

King Cole
A monarch noted for his slaw.

kinship
The family boat.

kitchen match
Marriage between the cook and bottle washer.

kith and kin
To show much affection.
Ex: I kith *(kiss)* her when I kin *(can)*.

KI-Ko

Kleenex
A daily nose-paper *(newspaper)*.

knapsack
Where the Sandman keeps his supplies.

knife sharpener
A man who is busiest when things are dullest.

knob
A thing to adore *(a door)*.

knotholes
Not holes.

knotting
Zero. Ex: I have knotting *(nothing)* to say.

knotty pine
The craziest tree.

know-how
Ability to speak an American Indian language.

kooky
A small, sweet cake that goes very well with milk. *(cookie)*

lacquer
(LAK-er) Be fond of a member of the female sex. Ex: I lacquer *(like her)* a lot.

lagoon
(lah-GOON) Slang for French gangster.

lamb stew
Much ado about mutton.

lap
What you lose every time you stand up.

Lapland
Thinly populated area in Northern Europe. There are not many Lapps *(laps)* to the mile.

Laplander
Someone who is unable to keep his balance on a crowded bus.

large-scale
What a fat person weighs on.

Lat-Le

lattice-work
What salads do for a living.

laughing stock
Cattle with a sense of humor.

launch
The meal most favored by astronauts. *(lunch)*

laundress
A gown worn for sitting on the grass. *(lawn dress)*

lava
(LAH-va) Have a strong feeling of affection for someone. Ex: I lava *(love)* you.

lawn
Grass à la mowed *(mode)*.

lawsuit
Uniform worn by a police officer.

lawyer
(1) Someone who prepares a 10,000 word document and calls it a brief. (2) Old lawyers never die, they just lose their appeal.

layer cake
A sweet food preferred by chickens.

lazy bones
A skeleton that doesn't like to work.

leading light
Star of Bethlehem.

leap year
The best time for a kangaroo.

legalize
What a judge sees with. *(legal eyes)*

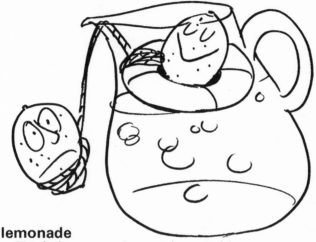

lemonade
To help out a lemon in trouble.

leopard
An animal easy to spot.

liability
(lye-uh-BIL-i-tee) The talent for telling untruths.
(lie-ability)

liberal
(LIB-er-al) A person who makes enemies left and
right.

Liberty Bell
A perfect name for someone who is half-cracked.

Lib-Lig

library
The tallest building in the world because it has the most stories.

lickety-split
To eat an ice cream dessert with bananas in it.

life
Life is like a shower: one wrong turn and you are in hot water.

life cycle
A bicycle you never outgrow.

light heavyweight
A boxer on a starvation diet.

lightning
The difference between lightning and electricity is that we have to pay for electricity.

light sleeper
Someone who sleeps on the chandelier.

likelihood
(LYKE-lee-hood) Probably a hat.

lilac
The ability to tell untruths. Ex: He's a nice kid, but he can lilac *(lie like)* a trooper.

Lincoln's Gettysburg Address
The last one on record is 128 Main Street.

liquor
(LIK-er) The ability to defeat a member of the female sex. Ex: I can liquor *(lick her)* any day of the week.

lisp
When you call a spade a thpade.

literacy
(LIT-er-a-see) To observe scattered rubbish. Ex: Your room is full of literacy *(litter, I see)*.

litter
Our grossest national product.

litterbug
A strew ball.

little things
It is the little things in life that annoy us: we can sit on a mountain but not on a tack.

livelihood
A perky gangster.

Ll-Lo

llama
Animall that eats llots and llots of llima beans.

loafers
Shoes for lazy people.

lobster
A sea creature that plays tennis.

local anesthetic
(LOH-cul an-es-THET-ik) Used in many operations. For those in a hurry, it might be better to take the express.

locate
A greeting for Kate. *(Lo, Kate!)*

lockjaw
What you get if you cross the Loch Ness monster with a shark.

locomotion
(loh-koh-MOH-shun) A really crazy dance.

locomotive
(loh-koh-MOH-tiv) A crazy reason for doing something.

locust
Swear under your breath. *(low cussed)*

Lone Star State
A country with only one actor in it.

long playing record
The most time anyone has ever lasted in a single game.

long puss
What a cat looks like after it has been run over by a steam roller.

long speech
A talk that can make you feel dumb on one end, numb on the other.

loquacious
(loh-KWAY-shus) Watch where you are going. Ex: She bumped into me, and I told her please to loquacious *(look where she was)* going.

Los Angeles Dodgers
Pedestrians in a large California city.

lots
What a real estate salesman has to know.

Lou-Ly

loudspeaker
Speechmaker who doesn't need a microphone.

love
Softening of the hearteries *(arteries)*.

loving cup
An affectionate piece of china.

lowbrow
A man whose toupee has slipped over his forehead.

low-down chiseler
A short sculptor.

lucky
The best key in the world to have.

lunatic
(LOO-nuh-tik) (1) A small blood-sucking insect that lives on the moon. (2) The sound your watch makes on the moon. *(lunar tick)*

lunge
The fencing master's favorite meal. *(lunch)*

lute
A stolen musical instrument. *(loot)*

lyceum
Where lice live.

lynx
(LINKS) What sausage comes in.

macaw
(ma-KAW) What I have trouble starting on cold mornings. *(my car)*

mahogany
(mah-HOG-a-nee) My missing pig. Ex: Someone stole Porky, and now I don't have mahogany *(my hog any)* more.

maiden
County of origin. Ex: My doll is maiden *(made in)* Japan.

mailbox
Where you would put letters to boys.

major
Forced you to do something. Ex: The alarm clock major *(made you)* get up early for a change, didn't it?

make-up exam
A test to find out how much you know about cosmetics.

Mal-Mas

məlign
(muh-LYNE) My side of the story. Ex: For some reason she didn't fall for malign (*my line*).

mammal
(MAM-al) Something that is neither fish nor fowl.

man
The only animal that goes to sleep when it is not sleepy and gets up when it is.

mania
(MAY-nee-a) Any large number. Ex: Mania (*many are*) called but few are chosen.

manor
(MAN-er) No living creature. Ex: This weather is fit for neither manor (*man nor*) beast.

marigold
Someone who weds for money.

maritime
(MAR-i-tyme) A fun-filled experience. Ex: A maritime (*merry time*) was had by all.

market
(MAR-kit) What a teacher does to a test paper.

Martian
A creature who is out of this world.

Mason-Dixon
Two gentlemen who knew where to draw the line.

Mayan

(MY-yin) A possession. Ex: What's yours is yours and what's Mayan *(mine)* is Mayan.

mayor

(MAY-er) A female horse. *(mare)*

meantime

(1) Nasty watch. (2) Hate *(eight)* o'clock.

meatball

Where butchers dance.

mechanize

(MEK-uh-nyze) Flirting. Who is he mechanize *(making eyes)* at?

meddler

(MED-ler) Someone whose business is none of his business.

Med-Meo

Mede
(meed) One man's Mede *(meat)* is another man's Persian *(poison)*.

Medea
(ma-DEE-a) A fond expression. Ex: Your slip is showing, Medea *(m' dear)*.

medieval
(mee-dee-EE-vuhl) Only half bad.

medicine show
Where pills go for entertainment.

melancholy
A fruit preferred by collies. *(melon collie)*

meow
A catty remark.

metaphor
   (MET-a-fawr) Have a date or appointment with a member of the female sex. Ex: I metaphor *(met her for)* lunch.

meteorite
   An expression of strong approval for a well-stuffed sandwich. Ex: This ham sandwich is meteorite *(meaty, all right)*.

meter maid
   A poetess.

metronome
   Hollywood elf. *(Metro gnome)*

microscope expert
   A person who magnifies everything.

midget
   Center engine of a three-engine jet airplane. *(midjet)*

Mil-Min

military dog
A West Pointer.

mind one's business
There are two reasons why some people don't mind their own business: (1) no mind; (2) no business.

mind reading
An easy thing to do—except where the print is too small.

Minerva
A jittery mental state. Ex: Minerva *(my nerves are)* shot from all the noise you're making.

miniature
(MIN-ee-uh-cher) A short period of time. Ex: Drink warm milk and you will fall asleep the miniature *(minute you're)* in bed.

minimum
A tiny English mother.

Minnehaha
(MIN-ee-hah-hah) Small laugh. *(mini ha-ha)*

minor operation
One performed on someone else.

mint
The most expensive flavor.

minute
To be positive. Ex: When I say something I minute *(mean it)*.

Minute Waltz
Music played by a watch band.

mischief
(MIS-chif) An Indian chief's daughter.

miser
(MY-zer) A person who lives poor so he can die rich.

misprint
Queen of the Press. *(Miss Print)*

missing link
A stolen sausage.

Mississippi
(mis-uh-SIP-ee) A hippie's wife. *(Mrs. Hippie)*

mistake
(mis-TAYK) A woman shoplifter.

Mist-Mo

mistletoe
(MIS-el-toh) What astronauts get instead of athlete's foot. *(missile toe)*

misty
Fail to catch. Ex: I misty *(missed the)* bus this morning.

mixed company
Confused business organization.

mobile home salesman
A wheel-estate dealer.

modern art
Oodles of doodles.

molasses
(moh-LAS-iz) Additional young girls.

money
(1) Money is often confused with dough. This is not correct, since dough sticks to your fingers.
(2) Money talks as much as ever, but what it says makes less cents these days.

money problem
A headache caused by asset *(acid)* indigestion.

monkey business
A swinging corporation.

moonbeams
What holds the moon up.

Moon-Mou

moonlighting
The sun's other job.

moralize
(MOR-ah-lyze) Fibs told for ethical reasons. *(moral lies)*

Moscow
(MOS-cow) Mother's pet milker. Ex: Moscow *(Ma's cow)* is next to Pa's cow.

mosquito
(muh-SKEE-toh) (1) An insect that makes you like flies better. (2) A flying hypodermic needle.

motel
(moh-TEL) William Tell's brother.

moth
An insect that enjoys chewing the rag.

mothball
(1) A moth in tears. (2) A dance for flying insects.

motorcycle
A vehicle that can't stand up by itself because it is two-tired *(too tired)*.

motorists
People who keep pedestrians in running order.

mountain climber
A person who wants to take just one more peak.

mountaineers
(mownt-uhn-EERS) How a mountain hears.

mountain range
A stove designed for use at high altitudes.

mouthwash
What you get for saying dirty words.

movie fans
(1) People who study the stars. (2) What cools a theatre in warm weather.

movie stars
People who work hard to become known and then wear sun glasses so that no one will know who they are.

mudpies
Organized grime.

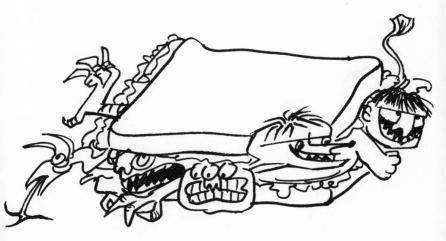

muenster cheese
(MUNS-ter cheez) Frankenstein's favorite sandwich. *(monster cheese)*

Muf-Mut

muffin
Frequently I am. Ex: I muffin *(I'm often)* grouchy in the morning.

mufflers
What keeps cars warm in winter.

muggy day
A day when everything that's supposed to stick together comes apart, and everything that's supposed to come apart sticks together.

mugwump
A bird that sits on a fence with his mug on one side and his wump on the other.

mumbo jumbo
A mute elephant.

musclebound
(MUS-el-bownd) Headed for the town of Muscle.

mushroom
The place where they store the school food.

musician
Someone who makes a living by playing around.

mutilate
(MYEW-ti-layt) A cat making noise after everyone's asleep. Ex: We could get more sleep if your cat didn't mutilate *(mew till late)*.

mutter
A parent of a mongrel dog.

mynah bird
(MY-nah bird) Any bird under 18 years of age. *(minor bird)*

mystic
How you can tell for sure that a clock is not wound up. *(missed tick)*

mystical
(MIS-ti-kul) What you call a ticklish lady. *(Miss Tickle)*

myth
A female moth.

nail
(1) A slender round object with a flat head which you aim at while you hit your thumb. (2) Some people cut their nails and throw them away; others file them carefully.

nail biting
A bad habit, especially if you are a carpenter.

nail polish
Finger paints.

Naval Academy
Belly Button University.

naval reserve
Spare belly buttons.

neck
Something that if you don't stick out in the first place, you won't get into trouble up to.

negative person
A nope addict.

neighborhood
The juvenile delinquent who lives next door.

nervous metal
Overwrought iron.

neurosis
(nyoo-ROH-sis) Fresh flowers that by any other name would smell just as sweet. *(new roses)*

neurotic
(nyoo-ROT-ik) A person in a clash by himself.

neurotic cow
An animal that suffers from a fodder *(father)* complex.

neuter
(NYOO-ter) A recent arrival. Ex: She must be neuter *(new to)* the class, because I never saw her before.

New-Nig

Newton's Law
One fig to every cookie.

night crawler
Sleepless baby.

nightingale
Very windy evening.

nightmare
A horse that keeps late hours.

night school
A school run by King Arthur for his men.
(knight school)

night watchman
One of those people who can make a living without doing a single day's work.

nitrate
(NYE-trayt) The cost of making a long distance phone call after dark. *(night rate)*

Nobel Prize
(noh-BEL PRYZ) An award given to those who have been without a bell for the longest period of time.

noble
(NOH-bl) Absolutely and completely true. *(no bull)*

noise pollution
The main cause of earitation *(irritation)*.

nominal
(NOM-i-nal) Very expensive. Ex: It costs nominal *(an arm and a)* leg for a new car these days.

nonsense
An elephant hanging over a cliff with his tail tied to a daisy.

nonstop talker
Someone who comes back from the seashore with a sunburned tongue.

noodle soup
Nourishment for the brain.

noon
A period of time spelled the same backwards and forwards.

normalize
(NOR-muh-lyze) 20–20 vision.

Not-Nu

noteworthy person
Someone who really knows the score.

noticeable
(NOH-tuh-se-bl) What you notice in the barn yard before you start running. *(notice a bull)*

notwithstanding
How to win a sitting contest.

nudnik
(NOOD-nik) A naked Santa Claus.

nuisance
Recently minted pennies. *(new cents)*

nursery
A child's ballroom *(bawl room)*.

Nutcracker Suite
A squirrel's hotel room.

oboe
(OH-boh) An ill wind that nobody blows good.

occident
(OKS-e-dent) What happens when two oxen collide.

occur
(a-KUR) A mongrel dog. *(a cur)*

ocean
(OH-shun) The place where buoys *(boys)* meet gulls *(girls)*.

ocelot
(AH-se-lot) A large amount. Ex: Ocelot *(that's a lot)* of money.

oddball
A strange round plaything.

office
(AH-fis) To arise from. Ex: I wish he'd get office *(off his)* chair and give me a hand.

Off-On

officiate
(uh-FISH-ee-ayt) Sea food eaten by a gentleman. Ex: He was ill from officiate *(a fish he ate)*.

Ohio
A friendly state because there is a "hi" in the middle of it.

ohm
There is no place like it.

"Oh, say, can you see?"
The eye doctor's theme song.

old comedians
Old comedians never die—they just gag a lot.

old hot rod
A shot rod.

Old Nick
A healed shaving cut.

old-timer
A grandfather clock.

olive
My place of residence. Ex: Olive *(I live)* up the block.

omelette
Share something with someone. Ex: Omelette *(I'm going to let)* you in on a secret.

one ton
(wun tun) A soup served in Chinese restaurants. *(wonton)*

onion
A food that may build you up physically, but will drag you down socially.

onyx
(AH-niks) Open and above board. *(honest)*

Open Door Policy
One way to keep your home cool without air conditioning.

open house
Home without a roof.

opening speech
What starts the bull rolling.

open mind
Some people think they have an open mind when it is merely vacant.

Ope-Opp

opera
A musical performance in which people sing before they die.

operator
Someone who hates operas. *(opera hater)*

operetta
A girl who works for the telephone company. *(operator)*

opinion
(uh-PIN-yon) Something you have on your mind and want to get off your chest.

opinionated person
(uh-PIN-yon-ay-ted PER-son) Like a steamboat, the more of a fog he is in, the louder he toots.

opportunity
It is supposed to knock, but it has never been known to turn the knob and walk in.

oppose
(a-POHZ) What people strike as they pass a mirror.

optimist
(OP-tim-ist) (1) A man who goes downstairs with a fish pole when he finds his basement flooded. (2) One who spends his last dollar to buy a money belt. (3) A person who goes into a restaurant with no money and figures on paying for his meal with the pearl he hopes to find in the oyster he plans to order.

orangeade
A fund for oranges in need.

orange
A fruit with a lot of appeal.

organ recital
A lecture about the heart, stomach, liver, lungs, kidneys, etc.

oriental fans
Chinese movie buffs.

Os-Ov

oscillator
(AHS-uh-lay-ter) Good-bye for now. *(I'll see you later.)*

osmosis
(oz-MOH-sis) How Moses introduced himself to Pharaoh. *(I'm Moses.)*

Ottoman
A car mechanic. *(auto man)*

ouch
The sound heard when two porcupines kiss.

outdoorsman
Someone who refuses to come in out of the rain.

out-of-bounds
A pooped kangaroo.

overdue doctor's bill
Long time no fee.

overeating
An activity that will make you thick *(sick)* to your stomach.

oversee
Any grade of B or better.

overture
At a place belonging to you. Ex: I'll see you overture *(over at your)* house.

P-Pa

P.A. system
A method used by fathers to raise children.

painless dentist
A dentist with an office that lacks windows. *(paneless dentist)*

palmist
Father's poor performance at the rifle range. *(pa missed)*

palomino
(pal-a-MEE-noh) A good friend of mine.

pancake
A waffle with the treads removed.

pancake make-up
To settle a fight over the breakfast table.

panhandler
(1) A plastic surgeon. (2) A dishwasher.

panther
A person who makes panths.

Pan-Par

pants
(1) Golfers wear two pairs of pants in case they get a hole in one. (2) In hot weather a man takes off his jacket, a dog just sits and pants.

parachute
Something that doesn't mean a thing, if you don't pull that string.

parachute jumper
A down-to-earth guy.

parachute school
A school in which you have to drop out in order to graduate.

paradise
Two ivory cubes with dots on them. *(pair of dice)*

paradox
(PAR-uh-doks) Two medical doctors. *(pair of docs)*

paralyze
Two untruths. *(pair of lies)*

parasite
(PAR-uh-syte) Someone who comes from Paris. *(Paris-ite)*

paratrooper
The only person who can climb down from a tree that he never climbed up.

parole
A word that makes sentences shorter.

parrot
  (1) Wordy birdy. (2) The only creature with the power of speech who is content to repeat what it hears without trying to make a good story of it.

pasteurize
  (PAS-che-ryze) Beyond what you can see. *(past your eyes)*

pastor
  To slip by. Ex: She was only a minister's daughter, but you couldn't get anything pastor *(past her)*.

Pat-Pe

patience
The ability to idle your engine when you feel like stripping your gears.

peace
An important part missing from the world.

peach
An apple in need of a shave.

peacock tail
A beautiful ending.

pea jacket
What a pea wears to keep warm.

peanut butter
A small billy goat.

pecan
Single out for special annoyance. Ex: Why don't you pecan *(pick on)* somebody your own size?

pedestrian
(pe-DES-tree-an) (1) A person who should be seen and not hurt. (2) There are two classes of pedestrians: the quick and the dead. (3) What the motorist is driving at.

pedigree
(PED-i-gree) A diploma awarded to dogs when they graduate from obedience school.

peephole
Members of the human race. Ex: Peephole *(people)* are funny.

pen
The pen is mightier than the sword, because no one has yet invented a ball point sword.

penguin
A bird that dresses formally on every occasion.

penmanship
A talent for getting along in jail.

Pennsylvania
(pen-sil-VAYN-ya) Where pencils come from.

pen pals
Pigs who are fond of each other.

perfect timing
Being able to turn off the "hot" and "cold" shower faucets at the same time.

Perf-Pes

perfume
(1) A gift that can cost a pretty scent. (2) An odor that leaves you smell-bound. (3) A best smeller.

perfume factory
A place where workers either make scents *(sense)* or they are fired.

perfume smuggling
A fragrant *(flagrant)* violation of the law.

period
A comma that has curled up and gone to sleep.

period costumes
Polka-dot dresses.

peroxide
(puh-ROK-syde) (1) Value of an oxhide. Ex: I'll give you twenty dollars peroxide *(per oxhide)*. (2) Teasing statement. Ex: Peroxide *(perhaps I)* did and peroxide didn't.

persecute
(PER-se-kyoot) An attractive little handbag.

personal foul
A chicken of your very own.

pessimist
(PES-i-mist) (1) A person who finds bad news in fortune cookies. (2) Someone who hangs around delicatessens because he is always expecting the wurst *(worst)*. (3) A person who looks at a doughnut and sees nothing but the hole.

pessimistic
(pes-i-MIS-tik) To walk by a guru. *(pass a mystic)*

petrified trees
(PE-truh-fyde trees) Trees that have been rocked by the rain and wind.

petty officer
A naval officer in charge of unimportant matters.

pharmacist
(FAHR-muh-sist) (1) The piller *(pillar)* of the community. (2) Short for a farmer's assistant. *(farm assist)*

pheasant under glass
(FEZ-unt) A small bird with a large bill.

Pho-Pi

phoenix
(FEE-niks) To turn down a sum of money. *(fee nix)*

phone book
A daring book. It actually names names!

photo finish
Graduation picture.

photographer
A confused person. First he asks you to smile, and then he snaps at you. The worst kind acts friendly enough, but then blows you up.

physician
(fi-ZISH-an) Someone who loses patients if he loses patience.

piano chord
What you tie a piano up with.

piccolo
(PIK-uh-loh) A musical pickle.

picket
Select something. *(pick it)*

pickle
A cucumber turned sour because of a jarring experience.

piemaker
A person whose job takes a lot of crust.

pig
An animal that has to be killed in order to be cured.

pigeon-hole
A bird's apartment.

pigeon-toed
A creature that is half bird and half toad.

piggy bank
Where pigs keep their money.

pigtail
A story about the three little pigs, for example. *(pig tale)*

Pilgrim
An unsmiling aspirin. *(pill grim)*

pilgrimage
(PIL-gri-maj) The age of the Pilgrims.

Pill-Pit

pill
A perfect nickname for someone who is hard to take.

pillow
Headquarters.

pilot's license
Fly paper.

pineapple
(PYE-nap-uhl) Fruit of the evergreen tree.

pink carnation
A country where all the cars are painted pink.

pins
Lost pins are hard to find because they are pointed in one direction but headed in another.

pioneer
(PYE-uh-neer) What a sloppy pie eater gets. *(pie in ear)*

pipecleaner
A long toothpick with a fur coat.

pipe dream
What plumbers have when they sleep.

pitched battle
Low-score baseball game.

pitcherful
What a baseball player says when he has just had a huge meal. *(pitcher full)*

plaintiff
(PLAYN-tif) An ordinary argument.

planet
The thing to do before you take a space trip.

playpen
A writing device used by dramatists.

playwright
(PLAY-ryte) Follow the game rules exactly.

plink
The color of a raindrop.

Plymouth Rock
Dance popular among the earlier settlers of the United States.

Pn-Po

pneumonia
(noo-MOHN-ya) Fresh, crisp paper bills. *(new money)*

pocket
What you do with your car when it is not being used. *(park it)*

pocket watch
A watch for people who don't like having time on their hands.

poetic license
Permission to write verse.

poets
(POH-ets) Writers who are usually poor, because rhyme does not pay.

point
To come to the point is to be blunt.

poise
(POYZ) When you raise your eyebrow instead of the roof.

poker
Something you do to a mule to get her to go. *(poke her)*

pole vault
(1) A bamboo safe. (2) Where Santa keeps his valuables.

policeman
Someone strong enough to hold up traffic with one hand.

policeman's ball
A cop hop.

policies
What a parrot does when it opens its eyes. *(Polly sees)*

politeness
Yawning with your mouth closed.

political candidate
A person who stands for what he thinks the people will fall for.

Polit-Poly

politician
(pahl-uh-TISH-un) (1) A kind of acrobat. He has to straddle the fence, keep his fingers on the pulse of the nation, point with pride, look to the future, and keep both ears to the ground. (2) A person who thinks twice before saying nothing.

politics
The most promising of all careers—promises, promises, promises . . .

poll taker
Someone who steals poles.

pollution
The dirtiest word in the world.

polyclinic
(PAHL-ee-klin-ik) A hospital for sick parrots. *(Polly clinic)*

Polyg-Pop

polygon
(PAHL-ee-gon) A disappearing parrot. *(Polly gone)*

polysyllables
(pahl-ee-SIL-a-blz) How a parrot speaks.

polyunsaturated
(pahl-ee-uhn-SACH-uh-ray-ted) A dry parrot.

Pony Express
The fastest way to ship young horses.

poodles
What you step into after it rains cats and dogs.
(puddles)

pop fly
A father insect.

popsicle
(POP-si-kl) Slush-ka-bob.

Popu-Pot

popular
One sure way to become popular is to breathe through your nose. This will keep your mouth shut.

populate
(POP-yoo-layt) What you say to your father when he oversleeps. *(Pop, you're late)*

porpoise
(PAW-pus) Do something for a reason. Ex: He did it on porpoise. *(purpose)*

positive person
(1) Someone who, finding himself in hot water, decides he may as well have a bath. (2) A person who, knowing the world is going to the dogs, starts a dog food factory.

postage stamp
A persistent piece of paper. It sticks to one thing until it gets there.

postman
A job that takes a lot of zip.

post office
Two words that have thousands of letters in them.

potholder
Someone clutching his belly.

pot roast
A sunburn on the stomach.

poverty
You know you are really poor when the only thing you can pay is attention.

power lawn mower
A motor sickle *(motorcycle)*.

power of deduction
The ability to reduce your income tax.

precedent
(PRES-a-dent) The elected leader of a country.

prehistoric times
The most widely read newspaper in the Stone Age.

prejudice
(PREJ-a-dis) Opinion without any visible means of support.

pressing engagement
Two tailors who plan to get married.

pressure cooker
Someone who works in a busy restaurant.

pretzel
(PRET-sel) A snack for someone with a twisted mind.

pretzel maker
The only person who makes crooked dough and is never arrested for it.

prickly pear
Two porcupines going steady.

Prince of Wales
The new baby in the house.

prism
(priz-um) A place where criminals are kept. *(prison)*

private eye
What you keep under an eye patch.

prize-fight
Disagreement over what's inside the crackerjack box.

problem
A harmonica player with chapped lips.

procrastinator
(proh-KRAS-te-nayt-er) A person with a wait *(weight)* problem.

program
To be in favor of the metric system. *(pro gram)*

propaganda
A socially correct male duck. *(proper gander)*

protein
(PRO-teen) To be in favor of adolescents.

proverb
(PROV-erb) A saying based on long experience. Ex: A soft answer turneth away wrath, but hath little effect on a door-to-door salesman.

prune
An old, wrinkled plum.

psychiatrist
(sy-KY-uh-trist) (1) A man who doesn't have to worry so long as other people do. (2) An ambivalence *(ambulance)* chaser. (3) A trauma *(drama)* critic.

Psy-Pu

psychoceramics
(sy-koh-ser-AM-iks) The study of cracked pots.

psychic
(SYE-kik) Someone who charges medium prices.

psychometrics
Mad measuring system

psychopath
Crazy road.

ptomaine
(toe-MAYN) A pterrible ptoxin causing ptremendous ptrouble in your ptummy.

public speaker
Someone who believes in a wordy *(worthy)* cause.

Pub-Py

public speaking
The art of making deep noises from the chest sound like important messages from the brain.

Puck
The character in Shakespeare who invented hockey.

Pulitzer Prize
(PUL-itz-er PRYZ) An award given to chickens for laying the smallest eggs. *(pullet-zer prize)*

pull
Something a dentist needs to be successful.

punch
A prize fighter's favorite drink.

puncture
A little hole in a tire usually found at a great distance from a garage.

punish
A play on words, sort of.

pupil
A pill that smells bad. *(pyew-pill)*

push-button warfare
An argument about who gets to use the pinball machine first.

pussy willow
A cat's I.O.U. *(pussy will owe)*

pyramid
(PIR-a-mid) A rock pile with a point.

Q-Qu

Q.T.
A pretty, young lady, for short. *(cutie)*

quack
A doctor who treats sick ducks.

quadruplets
Four *(for)* crying out loud.

quarterback
Your change from a dollar when you spend seventy-five cents.

quartz
There are four to a gallon.

quick-change artist
A supermarket clerk who can take your money, give you change, and sketch your portrait at the same time.

quota
(KWOH-ta) Report what a lady said in her own words. *(quote her)*

rabbit farm
A hare raising
(hair-raising)
place.

rabbit hole
Hare raid *(air raid)* shelter.

race horse
An oatsmobile.

racketeer
(rak-uh-TEER) A dishonest tennis player.

radioactive
A radio that moves around a lot.

Rad-Rap

radish
A shade of crimson. *(reddish)*

ragtime
When your clothes wear out.

raining cats and dogs
The weather when the dog catcher works the hardest.

raisin
A worried grape.

ransom
To move with speed. Ex: As soon as I saw the skunk, I ransom *(ran some)* distance away.

rap session
A mummy's convention.

rapture
(RAP-cher) Bundle your purchase. Ex: The clerk rapture *(wrapped your)* package with a bow.

rash prediction
Ex: "You will have measles."

ratify
(RAT-e-fye) To be a worse person for doing something. Ex: Will you think me a ratify *(rat if I)* tell the teacher?

raving beauty
A girl who thinks she was cheated in a beauty contest.

real estate salesman
Someone with lots on his mind.

Rec-Red

reckless
(REK-les) Someone who has driven a car for years without a single accident.

recoup
(ree-KOOP) To build up the chicken house after the chickens have flown.

rectangle
(REK-tang-l) A geometric shape that has been squashed. *(wrecked angle)*

red letter day
When the citizens of Moscow get their mail.

Red Riding Hood
A Russian tough guy pedaling a bicycle.

redskins
People who spend a day on the beach in the hot sun.

red tape
A kind of ribbon manufactured in Washington, D.C.

referral service
(ree-FUR-al SER-vis) Where an animal gets a new coat when his old one is worn out.

refuse
(ree-FYOOZ) What must be done when all the lights in the house go out.

reindeer
(RAYN-deer) What a mother raindrop calls its child. *(rain dear)*

relent
(ree-LENT) Loaned something out again.

relief
(ree-LEEF) What trees do each spring.

repairman
(ree-PAYR-man) The only happy person when things go wrong.

research
What you do when you can't find what you want in your bureau drawer.

retire
To fix a flat.

Retr-Ro

retrograde
(RE-troh-grayd) To get left back.

reverend
(REV-er-end) An unlimited time. Ex: If you
don't study, you'll be in this grade for reverend
(ever and) ever.

revolving door
A good place to meet people and go around with
them.

rhubarb
(ROO-barb) Celery with a sunburn.

rich milk
What you get if you feed cows money.

ringleader
First person in the bathtub.

ringside
Where you wait for a phone call.

river bank
Where fish keep their money.

roadbed
Where the highway sleeps.

road hog
A pig who hitch-hikes.

road map
Like a book of etiquette, it tells which fork to
use.

robin
A bird that steals.

rock and roll
Bulldozer's breakfast.

rock festival
A special celebration for geologists.

rocket
What you do to a baby to put it to sleep. *(rock it)*

rodeo performer
Someone who makes a living by throwing the bull.

roll call
Mating sound of a sesame seed bun.

Rom-Roy

Roman Empire
A sports official who travels around a good deal. *(roaming umpire)*

romantic cat
Smitten kitten.

rooster
An alarm cluck.

rope dancer
A talented piece of twine.

rotisserie
(roh-TIS-a-ree) A ferris wheel for chickens.

round robin
A chubby bird.

royalty
People who get their jobs through relatives.

R.S.V.P.
Short for: Rush in, Shake hands, Vanish Promptly.

rubber
The longest word in the dictionary because it can be stretched.

rubbish
Grime in the streets.

rumor
What is heard over the sour grapevine.

Running Water
A legendary American Indian chief. He is said to have had two daughters, Hot and Cold, and a son named Luke.

rural hamlet
A small pig that lives in the country.

Russian
To be courageous. Ex: Fools Russian *(rush in)* where angels fear to tread.

Russian dressing
A Muscovite putting on his pants.

rust
Metal *(mental)* illness.

saboteur
(sab-a-TOOR) A trip that spies take.

saccharin
(SAK-uh-rin) Where the game of soccer is played.
Ex: They play more saccharin *(soccer in)* Europe
than in the United States.

sadism
(SAD-izm) The science of being unhappy.

safari
(suh-FAR-ee) Up to this point. Ex: Safari *(so
far)* so good.

safe-cracker
A cookie that isn't dangerous.

safety
Everyone's cup of tea. *(safe tea)*

sailboat
A boat offered at a bargain price.

sailor
A wolf in ship's *(sheep's)* clothing.

sale
Where people go bye-bye.

Samson
The most popular actor in the Bible. He brought the house down.

sandwich
Seashore sorceress. *(sand witch)*

sapling
A young ignoramus.

sarong
(sa-RONG) What the teacher says to an incorrect answer.

Saturn
(SAT-urn) Reclined upon. Ex: Little Miss Muffet Saturn *(sat on)* a tuffet.

Sau-Sc

sauna bathers
Humid *(human)* beings.

savory
(SAYV-uh-ree) A non-commercial bank.

school board
The principal's paddle.

school spirit
Ghost that haunts a school.

scion
(SYE-un) To write your name. Ex: Please scion *(sign)* on the dotted line.

scorekeeper
A music librarian.

Scotland Yard
Two feet eleven inches.

scrap book
A book that tells you how to fight.

scratch paper
Paper that makes you feel itchy.

screen door
What kids get a big bang out of.

screen test
Something that insects are always trying to pass.

screwdriver
The nut behind the wheel.

sculptor
A chiseler. However, a sculptor who needs a bath is the worst kind, because he is a dirty chiseler.

Se-Sea

seafarer
The person who collects the fares on ocean voyages.

seaman
(SEE-man) A student whose average grade is "C."

seance
(SAY-ahns) Pronounce the word "aunt" in the plural. *(say "aunts")*

seashell
A torpedo.

seasickness
What a doctor does all day.

seasons
Everyone has a favorite season. Winter, however, leaves some people cold.

season tickets
Tickets the police hand out to bad drivers in order to save all that paper work.

seat belt
What you get if you stand too close to an irritated donkey.

secret
Something you tell to one person at a time.

secret service man
A garage mechanic in disguise.

seizure
(SEE-zher) To be able to tell. Ex: I can seizure *(see you're)* busy just now, so I'll come back later.

self-control
Saying, "No, thank you," when you want to yell, "Gimme!"

selfish
To retail sea food. Ex: This market would smell wonderful if it didn't selfish *(sell fish)*.

semiconductor
Someone who leads an orchestra once in a while.

senile
(SEE-nyle) Have a look at the most famous Egyptian river.

senseless
(SENS-les) Without a penny.

Sent-Ses

sentiment
   (SEN-ti-ment) What Santa Claus intended. Ex: Sentiment *(Santa meant)* to bring everyone toys this year, but he couldn't squeeze down all the chimneys.

sentry
   (SEN-tree) 100 years. *(century)*

serious discussion
   A case of mind over chatter.

serum
   (SEER-um) Note if any place is available. Ex: Do you serum *(see room)* for me in the lifeboat?

sesame
   (SES-uh-mee) I am doing the talking. Ex: Sesame *(says me)*, that's who!

setter
A breed of dogs often found hanging around bowling alleys.

sew and sew
A pair of tailors. A "dirty sew and sew," on the other hand, refers to a pair of unwashed tailors.

sewing circle
Where everyone gets needled.

sexes
There are three sexes: male, female, and insects.

shamrock
(SHAM-rock) A fake stone.

sheep dog
A dog that has moths rather than fleas.

sheer heaven
Where good hair goes after it has been cut.

sheet music
(1) What ghosts read to keep up with the latest tunes. (2) Music composed in bed.

sheik-to-sheik
A dance for Arabians.

shellacs
(shuh-LAKS) A flaw in her personality. Ex: Shellacs *(she lacks)* poise.

sherbet
(SHER-bet) A horse that can't lose. *(sure bet)*

She-Sho

Sherlock Holmes
A housing project outside of London. *(Sherlock Homes)*

shin
A keen sense organ that can find furniture, especially in the dark.

shoehorn
A musical instrument that plays footnotes.

shooting star
A famous actor who uses his gun too often.

shoplifter
Someone who lifts shops.

shortbread
(1) Melba toast. (2) Small salary. (3) Out of money.

short cut
A small wound.

shortening
One of the important ingredients in a good speech.

short wave radio
A radio with a crew cut.

shotgun
A worn-out firing piece.

show-off
A clear case of mistaken non-entity.

shutter bug
An insect that likes to take pictures.

shy person
Someone who must pull down the shade to change his mind.

sickbed
The perfect place for a sleeping pill.

sickle
Just a little bit sick.

sic transit gloria mundi
The transportation in this town is sick, but it will be better on Monday.

sideburns
What you get when your electric blanket is too hot.

Sid-Sk

sidewalk
Something that wears shoes but has no feet.

sight for sore eyes
A medical building for oculists, opticians and optometrists.

sign of spring
"Keep Off the Grass."

silicone
(SIL-uh-kohn) A dunce cap.

silo
(SYE-loh) A barely audible sound.

simpleton
Neither more nor less than 2,000 lbs.

sincere
Does awful things at this spot. *(sins here)*

sinew
(SIN-yoo) Observed. Ex: I sinew *(saw you)* at the movies last night.

sinus
(SYE-nus) Add our name to a list. Ex: Sinus *(sign us)* up for the team.

sit-down strike
A tack on your chair.

skeletons
A bunch of bones with the people scraped off.

skiing
A winter sport learned in the fall.

ski pants
Hard breathing heard on the slopes.

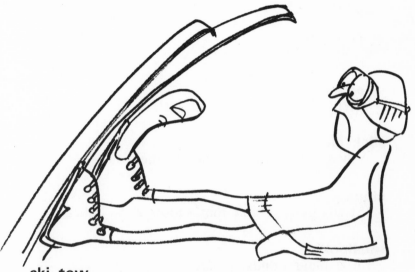

ski tow
(1) What skiers get instead of athlete's foot.
(2) Short for a nasty little bug that bites. *('squito)*

skittles
Very short plays. *(skits)*

skulduggery
(skul-DUG-er-ee) What undertakers do.

skylight
Sun, moon, or stars.

skyscraper
A device to clean up the atmosphere.

Sla-Sm

slapstick
A paddle.

sleep
Some people sleep like a log; others sound like a sawmill.

sleeping bag
A knapsack *(nap sack)*.

sleeping quarters
Twenty-five cent pieces at rest.

slick chick
A hen with grease on her feathers.

slogan
(SLOH-gun) A gun that shoots slow bullets.

smallpox
Little playgrounds. *(small parks)*

smarty-pants
Someone who carries a dictionary in his back pocket.

smash hit
A broken phonograph record.

smiles
(1) The longest word in the English language because there is a mile between the first and the last letters. (2) Curves that straighten most things out. (3) Inexpensive way to improve your looks.

snack
A refresher course.

snap, crackle, pop
The sound made by a firefly with a short circuit.

snapdragon
A long fire-breathing monster with a short temper.

snappy answers
What you would get if you crossed a telephone and a lobster.

sneakers
Footwear for spies.

sneeze
Much achoo about nothing.

snicker
A soft shoe with a cloth top and rubber soles. *(sneaker)*

Sno-So

snoop
Someone who believes there's no business like your business.

snoopers
The spies *(spice)* of life.

snoring
Sound sleeping.

snowball
Where snowflakes go to dance.

snowbank
Where Eskimos keep their savings.

snow job
Snowman's occupation.

soap and water
What makes criminals come clean.

soap opera
Singing while taking a bath.

soccer
To strike a member of the female sex. *(sock her)*

soda fountain
Newspapermen like to hang around them for scoops.

soda jerk
A licensed fizzician.

soft pedal
Slow going on a bicycle.

soggy noodle
What you get when you wash your hair.

somersault
Flavoring intended for use during July and August. *(summer salt)*

song bird
A bird that can give you a trill. *(thrill)*

song writer
(1) Someone who may not be able to carry a tune, but surely knows how to lift one. (2) A person who was calm and composed.

soot
What a chimney sweep wears. *(suit)*

sorcerer
(SAW-suh-rer) (1) Someone who works in a saucer factory. (2) Gravy chef. *(sauce-erer)*

Sord-Sp

sordid
(SAW-did) A strong expression of appreciation. Ex: I sordid *(sure did)* like that moving picture.

sore loser
A carpenter who misplaces one of his most important tools. *(saw loser)*

S.O.S.
(1) An expression of boredom, short for "Same-Old-Stuff." (2) A term in music: "Same-Only-Softer."

soul music
The sound made by squeaky shoes. *(sole music)*

soup
A food that should be seen and not heard.

sourball
A dance for lemons.

sourpuss
A cat that has swallowed a grapefruit.

South Pole
A place where many are cold *(called)*, but few are frozen *(chosen)*.

Soviet
(soh-vee-ET) We therefore dined. Ex: The waiter brought our food, Soviet *(so we ate)*.

spaghetti
A food discovered by a person who used his noodle.

specimen
Astronauts. *(spacemen)*

speechmaker
One who talks while others sleep.

spellbinder
A magician's looseleaf notebook.

spelling
The most important subject a young witch learns in school.

spelling bee
An insect that gets high grades in English.

spice
More than one spouse.

spinet
(SPIN-et) What a spider does with a web. *(spin it)*

spinster
An expert on tops.

spirit
Without spirit, you don't stand a ghost of a chance of doing anything.

spiritual lift
A haunted elevator.

spitting image
Disrespectful statue.

split personality
Someone who has slept on the railroad tracks.

splitting headache
The result of having an ax dropped on your skull.

splitting the atom
Ever since the atom was split, scientists have been wondering whether it was a wise crack.

spoiled children
The best way to prevent children from getting spoiled is to store them in the refrigerator.

spokesman
A person who talks like a big wheel.

spring cleaning
Removing dirt and dust from the inside of a watch.

springtime
What time it is when you sit on a tack.

square dance
Prom for people over thirty.

square meal
A box lunch.

square roots
(1) What a mathematician's plant has. (2) Diced beets.

squash racket
The illegal sale of squash.

stagecoach
A drama teacher.

Stag-Stat

stage manager
A Wells Fargo driver.

stained glass craft
A plane with streaky windows.

stalemate
A boring spouse.

stalk
What brings the little ears of corn. *(stork)*

Stamp Act
Temper tantrum.

stamping ground
The area around a post office.

standing army
Cheaper to maintain than a regular army because you don't need chairs.

starfish
A sea creature that comes out at night.

Stars and Stripes
The decoration of independence.

starship
A movie actor's yacht.

statesman
(1) A person who watches his appease and accuse *(p's and q's)*. (2) Someone who can be disarming, even though his country isn't.

214

statesmanship
The art of skating on thin ice without getting into deep water.

statistics
(sta-TIS-tiks) A bunch of numbers looking for an argument.

statuesque
(sta-choo-ESK) To request that someone repeat a question. Ex: What statuesque *('s that you ask?)*

steel wool
What gangster sheep do.

steering committee
Two backseat drivers.

stingy person
A person who won't even tip his hat.

stir-crazy
Mad chef's symptom.

Sto-Stor

stock exchange
A place where you trade in your old cattle.

stockholder
A corral for farm animals.

stole
What the burglar gave his wife for her birthday.

stomach
The home of the swallow.

stopper
To prevent a girl or woman from doing what she wants. Ex: She was only a bottlemaker's daughter, but nothing could stopper *(stop her)*.

story teller
A person who has a good memory and hopes other people haven't.

stowaway
(STOH-uh-way) A person aboard ship who never stops eating.

straight ruler
An honest monarch.

streaker
Someone who can run 100 yards in nothing flat.

striking personality
A prize fighter.

sturgeon
A fish that performs operations. *(surgeon)*

submarines
Sandwiches for underwater sailors.

subordinate clauses
(suh-BAW-den-it KLAWZ-ez) Santa's helpers.

subtitle
The name of a submarine.

subway motto
"The public be jammed!"

successful person
Someone who has learned the difference between itching for a thing and scratching for it.

sugar
Anyone who doesn't like sugar can lump it.

suit of armor
A knightgown.

Sum-Sup

summary
(SUM-er-ee) The weather during the hot months.

summer vacation
The bigger the summer vacation, the harder the fall.

sun
The oldest settler in the West.

sun and air
The male offspring who will inherit the family fortune. *(son and heir)*

sunbath
A fry *(fly)* in the ointment.

sunburn
Getting more than you basked for.

Sunday school
A place where they teach you how to make ice cream concoctions. *(Sundae school)*

sundial
What you use to tune in on the sun.

sunspots
Interplanetary measles.

superficial
Superman of the sea. *(Superfish)*

superior
(soo-PEER-ee-er) A very weird soup. *(soup eerier)*

supernatural
How monsters behave when they are relaxed and just themselves.

surfer
(SURF-er) Man over-board.

surgeon
(1) A big operator. (2) Like comedians, they keep people in stitches. (3) Old surgeons never die—they just cut out.

surrender
The knight of the Round Table who gave up. *(Sir Render)*

Surr-Sy

surround
(sir-ROWND) A short, fat knight. *(Sir Round)*

suspicious person
Someone who counts his fingers after shaking hands with you.

sweater
Something you put on when your mother gets cold.

sweepstakes
A lottery for janitors.

sweets
People who eat sweets end up with big seats.

swell
To see something swell, hit your thumb with a hammer.

swinger
A pendulum.

symphony
(SIM-fuh-nee) Appear to be amusing. Ex: Your jokes symphony *(seem funny)* to me, but I'll laugh at anything.

synonym
(SIN-uh-nim) A word you use when you can't spell the other word.

syntax
(SIN-taks) A fine for being naughty. *(sin tax)*

tact
The ability to get your point across without stabbing the other person with it.

tactful person
Ask him what his favorite color is and he will say, "Plaid."

take the rap
Hang up a guest's coat.

talebearer
Someone who can give you all of the details without knowing any of the facts.

talk
Talk is cheap because there is a good deal more supply than demand.

talkative people
People who must use gunpowder to brush their teeth, which is why they shoot off their mouths so much.

tangent
(TAN-jent) A man just back from a holiday at the beach.

Tan-Tat

tanker
The proper thing to do to a lady when she says something nice about you. *(thank her)*

tannery
The seashore.

tapeworm
What you get from eating cassettes.

Tarzan
The world's first swinger.

taste
The dieter's enemy because taste makes waist.

tattler
Someone who lets the chat out of the bag.

tattletale
(1) Someone with a good sense of rumor. (2) One who doesn't go without saying.

Tau-Te

tautology
(taw-TAH-la-jee) The study of education.

taxes
A bitter bill *(pill)* to swallow.

taxidermist
(TAK-si-DER-mist) A man who knows his stuff.

taxi driver
A man who makes a living by driving people away.

taxpayer
(1) The only person who doesn't have to take a civil service examination to work for the government. (2) Someone who has the entire government on his payroll.

tea
Break *(brake)* fluid for people.

tear jerker
Corn on the sob.

technical
(TEK-ni-kl) What a person does if you offer him five cents. *(take nickel)*

tee-hee
A male golfer.

teeny weeny
A rather small hot dog.

teeth
Be true to your teeth or they will be false to you.

Tel-Ten

telephone booth
A yak-in-the-box.

television
(1) Where movies retire in their old age. (2) Radio with eye strain. (3) What a prophet does. *(tell a vision)* (4) It is called a medium because anything good on it is rare.

television commercial
The pause that depresses.

television set
(1) Watching machine. (2) Boob-tube. (3) Vidiot's delight.

temper
The only thing you can lose and still have.

temporal
(TEM-per-al) The results of a person's excitable character. Ex: Your temporal *(temper will)* get you into big trouble one of these days.

ten acres
The result of wearing tight shoes. *(ten achers)*

tenderfoot
A vacationer on a dude ranch, although his foot is not exactly where he is apt to be tender.

tenderize
(TEN-der-eyez) An affectionate look.

Tennessee
(ten-a-SEE) The state where you can watch a lot of tennis matches.

tennis
(TEN-is) A noisy game because every player must raise a racket.

tequila.
(te-KEE-la) To murder a female. Ex: He never meant tequila *(to kill her)*.

terrarium
Where monsters work out.

terrible
Anything you can tear easily. *(tearable)*

terrier
A dog that makes you feel sad. Ex: One look at his hangdog eyes is sure to terrier *(tear your)* heart out.

Tes-Th

test pilot
Student who comes through exams with flying colors.

Teuton
(TOOT-un) To continue to play a musical instrument.

Teutonic
(too-TAH-nik) A 4,000 lb. Santa Claus.

Theophilus
(thee-AH-fah-lus) A name meaning something dreadful. Ex: There goes Theophilus *(the awfulest)* looking creature I ever saw.

Theory of Relativity
A theory about aunts, uncles, brothers, sisters, etc.

thermometer
An educated instrument because it has so many degrees.

thermos
There has to. Ex: Thermos *(there must)* be a better way.

thesaurus
(thi-SAW-rus) The tenderest. Ex: After riding a bronco, thesaurus *(the sorest)* part is where I sit.

thesis
(THEE-sis) The first word in a telephone conversation after "Hello." Ex: "Hello, thesis *(this is)* your old friend, Joe."

thinking cap
A headpiece worn by a skinny monarch. *(thin king cap)*

third degree
A diploma awarded to convicts.

thirsty
What may be found in the teapot. Ex: Help yourself, if thirsty *(there's tea)* left.

thirteen o'clock
Time to have your clock fixed.

The Three Little Bears.
A story about three nude midgets.

throng
Not correct. Ex: That's throng *(the wrong)* answer.

thumb tacks
A tax on hitch hikers.

Thum-To

thumber
(THUM-er) The warmeth theason. *(summer)*

Tibet
(ti-BET) To gamble on a sporting event.

Tibetan
(ti-BET-un) To go to sleep. Ex: Early Tibetan
(to bed and) early to rise.

time
An excellent healer but a poor beautician.

timid soul
A person who will leave pussyfoot prints on the
sands of time.

timpani
(TIM-puh-nee) A long musical composition.
Beethoven wrote nine of them. *(symphony)*

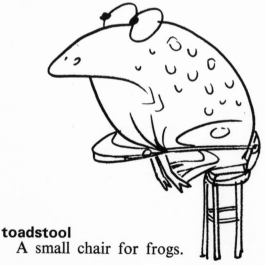

toadstool
A small chair for frogs.

toe dance
A ball for tow truck operators.

token
Speaking above a whisper. Ex: Token *(talking)* is not allowed in class.

tomorrow
One of the greatest labor-saving devices of today.

tom-tom
Two chaps named Thomas, for short.

tongue depressor
What makes your tongue feel sad.

Tong-Tor

tongue sandwich
Food that speaks for itself.

tongue twister
(1) A tornado with a hard-to-pronounce name.
(2) A group of words or phrases that get your tang all tongueled up.

tonsils
The part of the human body that has the best social life since it is taken out so often.

toothache
A pain that can drive you to extraction.

toothpaste
Helps to keep your teeth glued to your head.

top-secret
A top which few know how to spin.

torque
(TORK) To communicate by speech. Ex: Torque *(talk)* is cheap.

tortoise
(TAW-tus) What our teachers did.

tortuous
(TAW-choo-us) What you believe another person to be. Ex: I tortuous *(thought you were)* a good friend of mine.

totalize
A bunch of downright untruths. *(total lies)*

totter
(TAHT-er) To educate a female. Ex: I totter *(taught her)* everything she knows.

toucan
(TOU-kan) What a couple is able to do. Ex: Toucan *(two can)* live as cheaply as one.

touchable
Something that is basically true except for a bit here and there. *(touch of bull)*

tough luck
When you hope Lady Luck will knock on your door but her daughter, Miss Fortune *(misfortune)*, shows up instead.

Toup-Tr

toupee
(too-PAY) To whom you give your money. Ex: You have toupee *(to pay)* the piper.

towel factory
An absorbing place to work.

traffic light
A trick to get you halfway across the road before the cars start coming.

transaction
(tranz-AK-shun) Something done at a seance. *(trance action)*

transparent
Mother or father of the invisible man.

trapeze artist
Someone who won't last very long without the gift of grab.

treadmill
A factory where they make automobile tires.

treason
(TREE-zon) The male offspring of a tree. *(tree son)*

treble
(TREB-l) What musicians get into if they break the law.

tree lover
A person who leaves boxes of Kleenex under weeping willows.

tree surgeon
(TREE SER-jun) The only sort of doctor who can fall out of his patient.

tricycle
A tot rod.

trifle
(TRY-ful) A rifle with three barrels.

trouble
Opportunity knocks only once. Trouble is more persistent.

trousers
(TROW-zerz) An uncommon name—singular at the top and plural at the bottom.

Tru-Tur

truth
Stranger than fiction, but not as popular.

tuba
(TOO-bah) A small, collapsible cylinder of metal or plastic from which a semifluid substance can be squeezed. Ex: A tuba *(tube of)* toothpaste.

tulips
(TOO-lips) What you pucker up with.

tuna fish
Song about a sea creature. *(tune of fish)*

tunics
(TOO-niks) A couple of shaving cuts. *(two nicks)*

turkey
A bird that never eats on Thanksgiving because it is already stuffed.

turtle soup
A snappy dish.

"Tusk, tusk!"
What an elephant mother says when she scolds her baby elephant.

tutti frutti
(TOO-tee FROO-tee) A trumpet played by a fruit.

TV archeologist
The person who digs up the old movies for television.

TV dinner
A meal that comes complete except for the TV.

twirly
(TWER-lee) Much before a reasonable hour. Ex: It's twirly *(too early)* to get up.

twitch
A jittery sorceress.

two square feet
What a land surveyor stands on.

two-thirty
The time to visit your dentist. *(tooth-hurty)*

tyrant
(TY-rant) An insect dictator.

U-Un

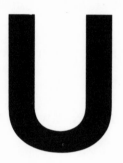

U.C.L.A.
What you can observe on a clear day in southern California. *(You see L.A.)*

ugly club
(UG-lee klub) A group of people who sing together as a chorus. *(a glee club)*

unaware
What you put on first and take off last. *(underwear)*

unbreakable toy
An object which is indestructible—until a child plays with it.

undercover agent
A spy in bed.

underground fighter
A subway rider during the rush hour.

underground garage
A wall-to-wall car pit.

undertaker
(1) A man who puts every customer in his place.
(2) A person who always carries out what he undertakes.

unfinished dictionary
A dictionary that stops at "nothing."

unhappy person
Someone whose life is just one big bed of neurosis. *(bed of roses)*

unit
Make me a woolen garment. *(you knit)*

university
(yoo-nuh-VER-suh-tee) A city in outer space.

unpleasant person
Someone who keeps you from feeling lonely, but makes you wish you were.

unwelcome visitor
One whose shortcoming is his long staying.

uppercut
(UP-er-kut) Meat from the top part of cow.

urchin
(ER-chin) The lower part of a woman's face. *(her chin)*

urgent
(ER-jent) Her boyfriend. *(her gent)*

used car
An automobile in first-crash condition.

vacation
A two-week period of rest that takes four weeks of rest to get over.

vain person
Someone who is always letting off esteem *(steam)*.

valuable
To set a price on a steer. *(value a bull)*

vanishing cream
What the invisible man puts in his coffee.

variant
(VAYR-ee-unt) A specific insect. Ex: That looks like the variant *(very ant)* that was here yesterday.

vegetarian
A salad *(solid)* citizen.

veneer
(ve-NEER) What you listen with. Ex: In veneer *(one ear)* and out the other.

venison

(VEN-i-son) When the light dawns. Ex: Venison *(when the sun)* comes up, the cock begins to crow.

venom

(VEN-um) How soon will it be. Ex: Venom *(when am)* I going to see you again?

verbatim

(ver-BAY-tim) Something used to catch a fish or other game. Ex: I use worms verbatim *(for bait)*.

vertigo

(VER-te-goh) In which direction did he head? Ex: He was just here, vertigo *(where did he go)*?

vicious circle

A round geometric figure with a nasty temper.

Vin-Vo

vine
A weak plant, since it can't even support itself.

violin
A dreadful little hotel. *(vile inn)*

violinists
The least serious of musicians. They are always fiddling around.

violins
Blood and gore. Ex: There is too much violins *(violence)* on television.

volcano
A mountain that has blown its stack.

Volga boatman
A crude, coarse seaman. *(vulgar boatman)*

waddle
Short for "what will you?" Ex: Waddle you give me to stop singing?

wafer
To be absent or missing. Ex: The cookie was sad because its mother was a wafer *(away for)* a long time.

wagging tail
A happy ending.

waiter
(1) A dish jockey. (2) A person who thinks money grows on trays *(trees)*.

waking up
A question of mind over mattress.

wallaby
(WAH-lah-bee) An expression of total surprise. Ex: Wallaby *(well, I'll be)* a monkey's uncle!

waltz
Anything belonging to Walter, for short. Ex: This is waltz waltz.

War-Wat

warrior
(WAW-ree-er) In what place. Ex: Warrior *(where have you)* been all my life?

Washington, D.C.
The city bureauful *(beautiful)*.

wastepaper
Dieter's gazette. *(waist paper)*

watchmaker
Someone who works overtime.

water bed
Where fish sleep.

water cooler
A thirst-aid machine.

watermark
An expression of surprise for a grade received. Ex: I didn't study and watermark *(what a mark)* I got!

watermelon
A fruit that you can eat, drink, and wash your face in at the same time.

water meter
Making the acquaintance of someone. Ex: She was only a plumber's assistant, but you water meter *(ought to meet her)*.

water-on-the-knee
The result of bouncing a baby on your lap.

watts
How you feel about a light bulb. Ex: I wike this wight bulb watts and watts *(lots and lots)*.

Watusi
(wah-TOO-see) Honest and aboveboard. Ex: Watusi *(What you see)* is what you get.

weakling
Someone who can't even carry a tune.

weather forecaster
(1) Someone who is always shooting the breeze.
(2) The only person who makes a living from guessing games.

wed
The color of marriage.

wedding ring
A one-man or one-woman band.

Wee-Wh

weekend
A poor football player. *(weak end)*

weird
Short for "where did?" Ex: Weird you meet her?

weirdo
(WEER-doh) (1) A strange looking deer. (2) A three-dollar bill.

well-informed person
Someone whose views are the same as yours.

well-seasoned traveler
A salt and pepper salesman.

well water
The best water to drink for your health.

wheeler dealer
An automobile tire salesman.

whey
(WAY) Route. Ex: Miss Muffet did not know where she was because she lost her whey.

whine
The sound let out by a grape when you squash it. *(wine)*

white rose
(ROZ) What White did when he sat on a tack. *(White rose)*

wholesale
Where holes are sold at a discount.

wholesome
The only thing from which you can take the whole and still have some left.

whooping cranes
Very excited lift machines.

wicker
Drained of energy. Ex: I feel wicker *(weaker)* when I don't have a good breakfast.

widow
How bread is made. *(with dough)*

wigwam
(WIG-wahm) A toupee in hot weather.

windbag
Someone who approaches every problem with an open mouth.

window
An amazing invention that allows you to see through solid walls.

Win-Woo

winter
A season so unpleasant, even the wind howls about it.

wire
Ask the reason. Ex: Wire *(why are)* you so nasty?

wise crack
An educated hole in the wall.

wisecracker
A smart cookie.

witchcraft
A flying broomstick.

witch's purse
Hag bag.

woe
(woh) The opposite of giddyup. *(whoa)*

wonder
(WUN-der) Reached first place. Ex: Who wonder *(won the)* race?

wooden nickel
An oaken token.

wooden shoe
(WUD-en SHOO) To inquire. Ex: Wooden shoe *(Wouldn't you)* like to know how I did it?

woodwork
It could come out as planned. Ex: It woodwork *(would work)* if you only tried.

woozy
Question about a stranger. Ex: Woozy *(who's he)* think he is?

world traveler
Someone whose mind wanders all over the place.

wrestle
(RES-l) The effect relaxation will have. Ex: The wrestle *(rest will)* do you good.

wrinkle
An area covered with ice. Ex: The skating wrinkle *(rink will)* be opened at noon.

wrist watch
A clock for people who don't like time on their hands.

write-in
A small period of time. Ex: O.K., I'll be write-in *(right in)*.

writing pad
A hippie author's apartment.

wrong
A word that if pronounced right is wrong, but if pronounced wrong, is right.

X-Xx

xenophobia
(zen-a-FOH-bee-ya) Observed no unusual fears.
(see no phobia)

xerophyte
(ZEER-a-fyte) There is no argument whatsoever.
(zero fight)

xerox
(ZEE-roks) To observe common hard materials.
(see rocks)

x-ray
Bellyvision.

XX
Treachery or betrayal. *(double-cross)*

yacht
(YAHT) Your duty. Ex: Yacht *(you ought)* to do as you are told.

yammer
(YAM-er) Refer to one's background. Ex: "Yammer *(I am a)* Yankee doodle dandy . . ."

Yank
A dentist of American extraction.

yardage
(YAHRD-ij) How old your lawn is.

yardstick
(YAHRD-stik) Something that has three feet but can't walk.

yawl
A boat used in the Southern part of the United States. *(you all)*

yawn
(1) An honest opinion openly expressed. (2) Things are always dullest before the yawn *(dawn)*.

Ye-Yy

yearnings
What you receive for working. *(earnings)*

yeller
The color of a cheerleader.

yellow pages
(1) Where the three little kittens found their mittens. (2) **A** telephone directory of cowards.

yes man
A person who stoops to concur *(conquer)*.

yesterday
To agree on the present date. Ex: Yesterday *(yes, today)* is the 28th of June.

yoga
The path you prefer. Ex: Yoga *(you go)* your way, I'll go mine.

yokel
(YOHK-l) Someone who laughs at yokes *(jokes)*.

YY
Overly smart or clever. *(too wise)*

zebra
(1) A horse with venetian blinds. (2) A sports model jackass.

zero
Usually the last row in the auditorium. *(Z-row)*

Zeus
(ZOOS) Where they keep caged animals.

zinc
(ZINK) Where one puts the dirty dishes.

zing
What you do with a zong. *(sing)*

zinnia
(ZIN-yuh) To be inside. Ex: How should I know what's zinnia *(in your)* mind?

zip
What the postman loses as he grows old.

zone
A personal preference. Ex: To each his zone *(own)*.

Zoo-Zu

zoo
 A place where people go and animals are barred.

zookeeper
 A critter sitter.

zoological
 (ZOO-loj-i-kl) Sloppy thinking. Ex: You are zoological *(so illogical)*: please follow the example of your head and come to the point.

Zuider Zee
 (ZEYE-der ZEE) (1) A gulf in zentral Netherlandz now zeparated by a dike from the North Zee. (2) An ocean of apple juice. *(cider sea)*

INDEX

253

255

256